Nuclear Strategy

The Doctrine of Just War

Attention Authors

Nuclear Strategy

The Doctrine of Just War

Sudha Raman

Manas Publications
New Delhi-110002 (INDIA)

Manas Publications
(Publishers, Distributors, Importers & Exporters)
4858, Prahlad Street,
24, Ansari Road, Darya Ganj,
New Delhi - 110 002 (INDIA)
Ph.: 23260783, 23265523:, 23842660 (R)
Fax: 011-23272766
E-mail: manaspublications@vsnl.com
Website: www.manaspublications.com

2006

ISBN 81-7049-269-6
Rs. 495/-

Typeset at
Manas Publications

Printed in India at
Salasar Imaging Systems, Delhi
and Published by Mrs Suman Lata for
Manas Publications, 4858, Prahlad Street,
24, Ansari Road, Darya Ganj,
New Delhi - 110 002 (INDIA)

Contents

Preface

The basic axioms of the nuclear weapons based international relations have been four: "impossibility of defence; vulnerability of cities; surprise attack and a capability of retaliation".

A study of nuclear strategy has always been for me an adrenalin for further knowledge and an area that provokes multitude of thoughts and ideas that transcend all boundaries that separate disciplines of thought, professions, churches, nations, religious and secular realms. "There is no issue at stake...", writes George F Kennan, "no hope, no fear, nothing to which we aspire, nothing we would like to avoid...which could conceivably be worth a nuclear war."

There continues to be search for ways to punish the aggressor in other ways than use nuclear weapons and without causing undue suffering, all the while remembering that fear and weight of armed superiority are the inherent qualities of human nature. "War in all its contemporary forms is insufficient to bring forth the exhaustion of all reasonable hopes of avoiding it."

Before the text of this book is imbibed by the reader, it is mandatory for me to state that ironically, much of what is said today as a new insight has been said already - maybe in a more sincere and effective manner. Hence most of the material is derivative. Finding alternate ways of expression was near impossible and hence the works of authors have often been referred to. I found it impossible to substitute their thoughts and expressions. My deepest gratitude to these writers.

The greatest danger, in my perception, that nations and its people face, is the utmost confidence and belief in the "absoluteness" of security. This sense of security was confined to the shelves with the atom bomb. The destructive power of the atom bomb also prompted, on an unprecedented scale, peace movements, scientists, strategists and even the Churches to break away from their normal routine and speak against the use of and the possession of this bomb.

The US strategic doctrine and the accompanying force structure have been built around nuclear weapons. The root cause of their security dilemma is clearly linked to the decision of post War American leadership resting security largely on technology – to compensate for the perceived Soviet superiority in manpower and conventional weapons – by relying on the dubious doctrine of nuclear deterrence and nuclear weapons. Nuclear deterrence became the ultimate national strategy and has remained unchanged in principle. Chapter One recounts the changing phases of nuclear deterrence.

Deterrence is the means to make nuclear employment unnecessary. An opponent would in fact say that nuclear weapons are largely a function of specific targeting strategies. Chapter Two details the targeting policies of the US in order to keep deterrence alive.

Deterrence is not primarily a military concept but an aspect of diplomacy. To be successful, it has to be based on weapons – but the ultimate success rests on non-use of the weapons. As Schelling has written, modern technology has enhanced the importance of "threats of war as techniques of influence, not of destruction; of coercion, of deterrence, not of conquest and defence, of bargaining and intimidation."

The threat of annihilation of this magnitude has given rise to moral concerns regarding the justness of the use of these weapons under any circumstances. The Just War forms the foundation for such protestations against the use of nuclear weapons. Chapter Three pertains to what exactly just war is.

The nuclear debate has provoked many people from different fields to question the morality of the very possession of these weapons and the threat to use them in case of necessity. Moral thinkers have upheld that not only must the cause of war be just but also the means used. This line of thinking prompted one of the most remarkable piece of judgement provided by the religious sect – the Pastoral Letter of the American Catholic Bishops. Chapter Four gives a brief analysis of this letter and a study of nuclear deterrence and national security based on the edifice of their letter. This is in fact an area of study that witnessed the most vociferous comments for and against the induction of nuclear weapons for the security of the US. According to James Turner Johnson, "Thinking about war in terms of just war tradition means allowing one's individual reflections to be guided by the experiences and reflections of others in a rich cultural history who have attempted to deal with practical problems both at the practice of war and at moral theorizing about war to 'keep faith' with this tradition."

The thesis concludes with a hope for a security set up that would not only help peace prevail but also sustain peace. The second aspect is what matters. After all "nuclear war can never be won and thus should never be fought."

Foremost, my deepest gratitude goes to my M.Phil as well as Ph.D Professor and Supervisor at Jawaharlal Nehru University, Professor Matinuzzaman Zuberi, whose strict training of research students brought the best out of them. His affection and patience is something to remember, and his knowledge something to aim for.

I would also like to state my deep appreciation for the help rendered in my research by His Grace, the former Archbishop Angelo Fernandes, Thirumeni Mar Gregarios, Reverend Arokyaswamy and Reverend Chatanat.

Air Commodore N B Singh welcomed me to his Institution – The United Service Institution of India – of which he was the then Deputy Director, and let me loose in the USI's marvellous library. This, in fact, was the beginning of the wonderful nine years of my working life. I now am the Research Coordinator in the USI's research section.

The other libraries that have been of great value are of my own JNU, the Institute for Defence Studies and Analyses, the American Centre, and the Vidyajyoti Publications.

My mother has been the pillar of all my endeavours. She bore the brunt of my long hours of research and continues to strengthen my desire for more knowledge. So, to just say thank you to her would be a grave mistake. I know she will understand what I wish to say.

Once again, I have been very fortunate indeed to have completed my Doctorate under the supervision of Professor Zuberi and to have also interacted with his equally wonderful wife, Mrs Nasreen Zuberi.

Sudha Raman

1

Nuclear Deterrence

The very purpose of deterrence is to deter a nuclear and conventional attack on the territory of a state, of allies, and friendly neutrals. And, credibility is the additive of effective deterrence. The dilemma arises when the search begins for the absolute means to provide foolproof deterrence. Herein lies the incisive point in what the aggressor believes and what he actually implements. "Deterrence", Henry Kissinger once remarked, "occurs above all in the minds of men."[1] The psychological framework of deterrence decides the behaviour of the deterer and the deterred.[2]

Nuclear deterrence, in fact, has been referred to as "a policy and as a situation." It has the ability to not only prevent a major war but also limit the area of conflict while using the threat to avoid it in other areas. A deterrent situation, thus, is one where conflict is contained within the boundary of threats which are neither executed nor tested.[3]

---

1. Henry Kissinger, *American Foreign Policy* (New York: WW Norton, 1974), p.15.
2. Robert Jervis, *The Illogic of American Nuclear Strategy* (New York: Cornell University Press, 1984), pp. 37-40.
3. Roy E Jones, *Nuclear Deterrence: A Short Political Analysis* (London: Routledge and Kegan Paul, 1968), p.1.

There is a succinct difference between deterrence and defence. Deterrence denotes a policy of dissuasion based on threatening results that would outweigh the benefits hoped for. Defence is a policy of dissuasion based on counter-posing forces so that an attack would fail. Defence comes into force when a war begins; deterrence is to prevent a war from breaking out. Once an offensive is in operation, defence tactics take over, and deterrence fails.[4] States normally attempt to deter by defensive methods. And a perfect defence is an excellent deterrent.[5] It is a general presumption that when defence is weak, offensive technology is the more tempting option. Any improvement in defence reduces the incentive to attack, but forces the adversary to improve their own defence, prompting in the process an arms race. This also entails prompting of development of nuclear weapons. After all an effective nuclear deterrence requires sufficient nuclear capability. Planning to prevail in a nuclear war is the aim of deterrence as the potential adversary has to be convinced of the retaliatory capability of the deterrer.[6]

In the conventional sphere, the superiority of the defensive over the offensive capabilities promoted stability. This is the essence of dissuasion through defence. Thus, deterrence and defence, though analytically different, are interrelated. Unfortunately, nuclear weapons can deter but

4. David W Ziegler, *War, Peace and International Politics*, 2nd Edn (Boston: Little Brown, 1981), p.227.
5. Glenn Snyder, *Deterrence and Defence: Towards a Theory of National Security*, (Princeton N.J.: Princeton University Press, 1961), pp.3-15 and David Bobrow, (ed), "Deterrence by Denial and Punishment", in Bobrow, *Components of Defense Policy* (Chicago: Rand McNally, 1965), pp. 209-237.
6. Donald Brennan, "The Case for Missile Defence", *Foreign Affairs*, Vol.47, No.3 (April 1969), pp.440-441 in Patrick Morgan, *Deterrence: The Conceptual Analysis* (UK: Sage, 1977), p. 32.

cannot defend. Thus, the central problem of deterrence is that its consequences of failure are not acceptable.[7]

There is a distinction between deterrence and compellence too; the latter being a threat of force to make the other party do something or undo something already done.[8] Compellence may not be solicited for aggressive purposes. Compellence, as Schelling would have us believe, is harder to achieve, is more complex and certainly more dangerous when it involves the threat to use nuclear weapons. It could be attempted in unusual and extreme circumstances and it carries a high probability of failure unless the conditions are right.[9] Comprehending the strategic implications of the advent of nuclear weapons, Bernard Brodie, in 1946, formulated the first framework of the doctrine of nuclear deterrence. He observed thus: "Thus far the chief purpose of our military establishment has been to win wars. From now on its chief purpose must be to avert them. It can have no other useful purpose."[10]

Deterrence is grounded on four conditions:[11] the state engaged in deterrence must have the *capability* to ensure that the political adversaries will profit less by going to war than by refraining from war. In order to preserve the deterrent capability the state must be able to deliver nuclear capability

---

7. Keith B Payne and Colin S Gray, "Nuclear Policy and the Defensive Transition", *Foreign Affairs*, Vol.62, No.4 (Spring 1984), pp.822-823.
8. Thomas Schelling, *Arms and Influence* (New Haven, Conn: Yale University Press, 1966), pp.69-91.
9. George Alexander, David Hall & William Simons, *The Limits of Coercive Diplomacy* (Boston: Little Brown, 1971).
10. Bernard Brodie, *War and Politics* (London: Cassell, 1973) and his book *The Absolute Weapon : Atomic Power and the World Order* (New York: Harcourt Brace, 1946).
11. It is interesting to read Gp Capt Timothy Garden's assessment in *Can Deterrence Last: Peace Through a Nuclear Strategy* (London: Buchan & Emight Publishers, 1984).

under all possible circumstances. The deterrent state must have the *will* to use the capability if necessary. This necessitates a secure command and control system and a general state of readiness of the nuclear weapons stockpile. These arrangements also demand targeting policies and deployment of nuclear warheads and delivery systems in a way that will deliver the warheads of the target specified at the appointed time. Flexible response, counter-force and counter-value strategies form part of this effort. The adversary must be convinced of the capabilities and the will of the deterring state. A convincing readiness to fight the nuclear war at any level is essential to ensure such *credibility*.[12] Civil defence measures and the complete integration of the nuclear forces into the battle plans are supposed to make deterrence posture more credible. Not only must nuclear forces be invulnerable, the potential adversary must consider as true that they are. "Deterrence cannot be too timid to lose credibility or too vigorous to promote war." Professor Thomas Schelling writes of manipulations of credibility as a means towards greater deterrence.[13] The centre-piece of US deterrence is the *rationality* of the leaders of the nuclear weapon states. They are supposed to make a rational calculus of costs and benefits of their policies. Steinbrunner points out the irrationality of carrying out the threat on which the policy of deterrence is based – should deterrence fail and war begin. It is assumed that no rational decision-maker would provoke a nuclear war because there do not seem to be any conceivable objectives of a state that can be attained by the use of nuclear weapons.[14] The First World War, a war

12. John Herz, *International Politics in the Atomic Age* (New York: Harpers, 1981).
13. Thomas Schelling, *The Strategy of Conflict* (Cambridge, MA.: Harvard University Press, 1960), p.187.
14. John Steinbrunner, "Beyond Rational Deterrence: The Struggle for New Conceptions", *World Politics* (January 1976), pp.223-245, at p.241.

that no one wanted,[15] is a classic example of how a war can start irrationally. It was a war that was initiated by circumstances that were trivial yet out of control.[16] Stress and time pressure took their toll in turn. The Cuban missile crisis would have shown entirely different results but for the fact that the Kennedy administration had both these vital aspects to their benefit. The absence of a rational basis for retaliation, according to Morgan, if deterrence fails, would guarantee no disincentive to the opponent who considers attacking. After all, what may seem rational to some may seem irrational to others.[17] A certain level of rationality is presumed in the decision-making process of that state which has to be deterred for deterrence to be successful. The punishments to be endured in a nuclear retaliation are expected to impose a certain caution in the behaviour of the states married in a nuclear deterrence relationship. When mutual deterrence is in operation, a similar assumption about rationality of decision-makers is implicit in the working of this posture.[18]

The dilemma begins when it is realised that it is most irrational to carry out the retaliatory second strike, if deterrence has failed, because the retaliator will also suffer incalculable losses. If the carrying out of the threat is irrational and there is an assumption of rationality, then the threat will not deter. Deterrence would fail in those circumstances. Morgan summarises this predicament thus: "The ultimate problem in devising a theory of deterrence is to simultaneously postulate that officials in government are

---

15. Herman Kahn's observations in Philip Green's *Deadly Logic: The Theory of Nuclear Deterrence* (Columbia: Ohio University Press, 1966), p.206.
16. P H Hinsley, *Power and the Pursuit of Peace* (London: Cambridge University Press, 1963), p.286.
17. Steinbrunner, n.14, pp.233-245.
18. Garden, n.11.

sometimes in some ways conscious and rational, yet take into account that certain forces work to make their behaviour unconscious and irrational.[19]

Deterrence, thus, operates on the rational fear that the adversary will act less than rationally, once it has suffered severe losses. The enormity of stakes involved in a nuclear war for our society ensures that the process by which nuclear weapons might come to be used, stimulate vast and varied debates of concern for the consequences in the event of such an outcome. The question of how, when and why to use nuclear weapons remains a matter of conjecture. Henry Stimson, Secretary of War from 1940- 1945, made it clear that the common objective throughout the war was to first produce an atomic weapon and use it. On no other ground could so much time and expenditure be justified.[20]

Security of the United States and the Two World Wars

Nuclear deterrence evolved as an intellectual construct in the late 1950s and early 1960s. But the dilemma in the US national security is that it is less secure today than it was before – a situation created by technological advances, independent choices of decisions of America's allies and American choices of strategy and policy. Until the 20th century, war had its own place – momentous and yet secondary. It was never a threat that was sought or felt. The gradual emergence of a system of politics of any one nation or group of nations balanced against each other, in Europe, reached its zenith in the 19th century when the Congress of Vienna redrew the map of Europe to avoid concentration of power at any one place. The 'Concert of Europe' – an agreement amongst great powers to pursue

19. Morgan, n.6, p.102.
20. Henry Stimson and McGeorge Bundy, *On Active Service in Peace and War* (London: Hutchinson, 1948), p.361.

national interest within the realms of interest of the system as a totality and hold international congresses rather than go to war – was created. The phase of industrialisation, however, altered the science of war, culminating in a race among the few to outstrip the already 'owned' areas. Both the World Wars were the result of imbalance in this power relationship in Europe.

In the words of Raymond Aron, with World War I began the century of total war, a century when even in peacetime, preparations for war and national security claimed "priority in resource utilisation over social and economic development. This is a century when the world is balanced between war and peace – we win if we don't fight and if we lose we are not there to be perturbed by our conscience."[21]

Liddell Hart has rightly said that "strategy is the art of distributing and applying military means to fulfil ends of policy", stressing the role of political sphere as the source· of strategic objective.[22] The US's potential to be a power to be reckoned with was tested for the first time in 1917, as she sent a modest force to France to help the exhausted European nations to reach a victorious outcome in World War I, in a short duration. The First World War was witness to the most terrible slaughter as rivals tried to penetrate the defenses of the other involving the whole society – in victory and destruction. Success depended on the numerical and industrial strength of nations and the two sides were engaged in exhausting each other's

21. For an excellent analysis and detailed assessment, see R Smoke, *National Security and the Nuclear Dilemma* (Reading, MA : Addison-Wesley Publishing Co., 1984) & John C Campbell, *The U.S. in World Affairs : 1948-1949* (New York : Harper & Row, 1949).
22. Basil Liddell Hart, *Strategy: The Indirect Approach* (London: Faber & Faber, 1968), p. 334. Strategy is from the Greek word 'Strategos', i.e., the art of the General. General Carl von Clausewitz (1780-1831) defined it as the use of battle to forward the aim of war.

prime resources and human lives. The results were slow and demanded a great amount of forbearance and level headedness, resulting in search for new ways to achieve a conclusive victory quickly. A solution was soon found in the use of tanks and aircraft – it compensated well for the need for mobility of weapons though it was as yet untapped for full utilisation. The doctrine of strategic bombardment provided for the most effective use of aircraft to attack the social and industrial bases of the enemy by pre-emptive strike on air bases, "without formal declaration of war to bring a moral and material collapse."[23] This belief in the effectiveness of the 'first blow' is due to the identification of morale as the critical determinant in warfare. Clausewitz described physical force as the wooden hilt of the sword while moral force was the shining blade. The United States has enjoyed this unique position of superiority at hardly any cost to itself – situated away from all problem states and protected by the oceans. This power position reached its pinnacle in the first half of the 20th century.

From 1940-1945, the US underwent a profound change. It created a large armed force, mobilised its human and material resources for the prosecution of war, and even harnessed the energy trapped in the atom for military purposes. They exercised restraint at the start of World War II[24]. Interestingly, Hitler himself had laid down a guiding action on the part of Germany. This got eroded after the fall of France. The failure to utilise air power as a military and discriminatory instrument could be blamed on the technological inaccuracies and proximity of the civilian areas to military targets, with no rigid boundaries specifying a combat zone.

---

23. Giulio Douhet, *The Command of the Air,* trans, Ding Ferrari & Lawrence David (New York : Coward-McCann Inc., 1942), p.220 in Lawrence Freedman, *The Evolution of Nuclear Strategy* (London : Macmillan, 1981), p.7.
24. Donald Cameron Watt, "Restraints on War in the Air Before 1945", in Michael Howard (ed)., *Restraints on War : Studies in the Limitation of Armed Conflict* (London : Oxford University Press, 1979).

In fact, the very first year of the War demonstrated the limitations in the effectiveness of air power. While the Luftwaffe destroyed the air bases of the British Air Force and struck the civilian population, there was an underestimation of civilian morale and an overestimation of air defence.

The introduction of nuclear weapons created a wholly unprecedented situation, rendering all previous strategic theories and concepts immediately obsolete. Ironically, these weapons were created by a fear of consequences of a unilateral German success in the military exploitation of the atomic energy.[25] The strategic use of the bomb was determined by the conditions then prevailing. By mid 1945, Japan was a spent force and the problem for America was to get Japan to surrender unconditionally and end the war quickly. It was, thus, necessary to emphasise the uniqueness and awesome destructive power of the bomb and, in the words of General Leslie Groves, adversely effect the will of the Japanese people to continue the war[26] by a surprise attack.[27] The atomic bomb was to be a psychological weapon.[28]

The decisive effect of nuclear weapons was undisputed at this stage.[29] The nuclear bomb did accelerate the speed of termination of war. It re-strengthened the argument in favour of effective strategic bombardment.[30]

---

25. History would have been different had Germany made the bomb.
26. Leslie R Groves, *Now It Can Be Told : The Story of the Manhattan Project* (New York : Harper, 1962), p. 267. The principal influences on the use of the bomb were Stimson, Groves, Marshall, Connant and Oppenheimer.
27. L Giovannitti, & F Freed, *The Decision to Drop the Bomb* (London: Methuen & Co., 1967), p. 35 & Basil Liddell Hart, *The Revolution in Warfare* (London : Faber & Faber, 1946), p. 25.
28. Stimson & Bundy, n 20, pp. 36, 370, 373
29. Hart, n. 22, pp. 30-32.
30. November 1945, Final Report by Secretary of War – General Arnold, Chief of Air Staff; see Freedman, n. 23, p. 23.

The Policy of Containment

The onset of the Cold War saw the United States evolve a policy of 'containment' of the Soviet Union.[31] The policy had military implications but it was not clear what military resources might be needed to sustain containment, what military threats might be encountered and how they might be met. For Kennan, who propounded the concept, containment was not just the prevention of Soviet expansion but a way to create awareness of the benefits of long term peace. Once this awareness was imbibed by Soviet leaders the utility of containment would end. Kennan opposed the harsher features that containment developed with the deepening crisis of the Cold War.[32] Military containment was extended to the Far East – where the circumstances were far removed from those in Europe.[33]

Nuclear Deterrence

While containment became the central theme of US foreign policy, the Western powers had little conventional military power in comparison to the vast Soviet Red Army, but the US was the only nation that had the atomic bombs. American strategy at this point was to deter the outbreak of a new war by threatening destruction of the Soviet homeland if the Soviets were to seize Western Europe. The strategy played to America's strength and Russia's weakness. The Soviet leadership would

31. John L Gaddis, *Strategies of Containment : A Critical Appraisal of Post War American National Security Policy* (New York : Oxford University Press, 1982). For a succinct understanding of this subject see the RAND publication by Mark Dean Millot, "The Role of Deterrence in America's European Strategy", *RAND N - 3183-AF* (March 10, 1992), pp. 3-6.
32. For a critical appraisal of military containment, see George F Kennan, *The Nuclear Delusion : Soviet and American Relations in the Atomic Age* (New York : Pantheon, 1982).
33. R Smoke, n. 21, p.52. Later Kennan specified that he meant political and not military containment of Soviet power.

not attack Western Europe due to fear of a retaliatory strike. The nuclear threat need never be carried out.[34] As a strategy, deterrence seemed to be straightforward and uncomplicated. Nobody knew whether it would work or not.[35]

Containment and deterrence reigned supreme in their own spheres. The former was pursued by political and economic means and the latter by the US Strategic Air Command (SAC). However, the strength of Soviet conventional forces in Central Europe was exaggerated.[36] The strategy of nuclear deterrence was an "empty threat" in the early post War period for the US did not have sufficient bombs to carry out the threat. In the following years two events shaped American foreign and security policies, which determined the contours of international politics and relationships for more than four decades – the Communist takeover of China and the first Soviet atomic test announced by the United States on September 23, 1949.

The Americans took to "Operation Skywatch" to scan the sky for incoming bombers. They hadn't expected Soviet Union to catch up with US so soon. Not surprisingly, the blending of ideology and the atom bomb implanted a sense of fear in the minds of the Americans regarding the next step that the Communists would take. After all, they ruled one fourth of the world's population and controlled most of the earth's landmass. It is at this time that Truman ordered a complete review and re-analysis of the US national security affairs. He decreed that the US Defence Department further

---

34. B M Russett, "The Doctrine of Deterrence", in Philip J Murnion, *Catholics and Nuclear War : A Commentary on the Challenge of Peace : The US Catholic Bishops Pastoral Letter on War and Peace* (New York : Crossroads Publishing Co., 1983).
35. Bernard Brodie, *The Absolute Weapon,* n.10 Brodie challenged the notion of victory as resting on numerical superiority.
36. Thomas W Wolfe, *Soviet Power and Europe 1945 - 1970* (Baltimore: John Hopkins University Press, 1970), p. 10.

the development of a more terrible nuclear weapon that was now possible (code named "Super").[37] This culminated in the explosion of a hydrogen device in the Pacific Islands in 1952.[38]

National Security Council (N.S.C.) - 68

The National Security Council analysed the challenge posed to American security and submitted four options in April 1950.[39] A comprehensive national security policy and a general strategy[40], proposed by Paul Nitze, the four options were :-

a) To continue policies then being pursued.

b) Revert to isolationism and defend just the West.

c) To launch a "preventive war."[41]

d) To build up American power.[42]

The last point gained currency – a build up was necessary to deter Soviet or Soviet directed actions. The need was also

37. D E Lilienthal, *The Journals of David E. Lilienthal* (New York: Praeger, 1964), pp. 581 & 591.
38. Decided on January 31, 1950. David A Rosenberg, "American Atomic Strategy and the Hydrogen Bomb Decision", *Journal of American History* (June 1979), pp. 62-87.
39. Refer Samuel F Wells, Jr, "Sounding the Toxin : NSC-68 and the Soviet Threat", *International Security* 4, pp. 116-158 for the drafting of NSC-68 and assessment of its context.
40. NSC-68 was published in *Naval War College Review*, Vol. 27, pp. 51-108.
41. Truman's farewell address stated as unthinkable for a rational man, the starting of an atomic war. Quoted in Gregg Herken, *Councils of War* (New York: Alfred Knopf, 1985), pp. 94-95. Eisenhower opines the same view on "Developments in East Europe and the Middle East", *Department of State Bulletin*, October 12, 1956, pp. 743-745 quoted in "Eastern Europe and the Soviet Union" in Walter La Feber (ed), *The Dynamics of World Power: A Documentary History of US Foreign Policy 1945-1973*. Vol.2. (New York : McGraw Hill Publication 1973), pp. 558-559.
42. Smoke, n.21, p.59.

felt for developing an adequate defence against air attack on the US along with a defence against air and surface attacks on the UK and Western Europe. NSC-68 set out categorically, the relations of power and the will to use force. Without a superior military strength, politics of containment - based on gradual coercion – would be no more than a policy of bluff. The document called for the need to corrode the legitimacy of the nuclear role of the Soviet Union over Eastern Europe as also in the other areas under its control. This policy was termed "rollback", during the period of Dulles. And, it replaced containment. It recommended defence against air attack towards which no efforts had been made until then. This was one specific recommendation of NSC-68 which was carried out. However, a Soviet invasion of Western Europe meant an all out war with Soviets in a position to counter attack. The nuclear forces were now beginning to be seen as mutually pushing them towards a nuclear stalemate. The search for a course to protect their European allies, cleared the way for the US for a conventional build up. The idea was that the US forces would serve as a tripwire not as a force providing man for man against the Red Army – a force large enough to affirm its determination to defend Europe and make any invasion/ attack costly for the Soviets to contemplate. For this, NATO would also have to contribute forces.[43] However, NATO allies could not shoulder this burden by 1954 as it meant large US armed forces and air force commitment in Europe along with adequate naval protection of its supply line to and from Europe.

With the Soviet Union going 'nuclear', the assumption that deterrence was automatic, ended.[44] Deterrence, a vital policy

---

43. Honore M Catudal, *Nuclear Deterrence : Does It Deter?* (New York: Mansell Publication Ltd., 1985), p. 94.
44. Henry Kissinger, *Nuclear Weapons and Foreign Policy* (New York: Harper and Bros., 1957). This book made the first major attempt to rethink American foreign policy on the premise that the Soviet Union had attained the capacity to destroy American cities.

objective became an enigma that could not be abandoned nor pursued with a clear limit of its effective duration.

However, before the policy advocated in NSC-68 could be adopted, the US was involved in the Korean War. The American conventional and nuclear weapons policy followed the outbreak of the Korean War and gradually led to the articulation of a strategy of nuclear deterrence. The principal difficulty one came across while assessing the policy of deterrence was the belief that deterrence was a relatively straightforward thing. The meaning is simple and straight sure enough, but finding the best way to threaten it and how to punish the adversary if it failed, ie the right means for implementing it, were the complications involved.[45]

The New Look Policy

It must not be overlooked that 1950s was the era of American military superiority. Interestingly, while the US was riding high on a rapidly improving air defense system including radar stations across Canada, jet interceptors, ground launched aircraft missile ('Nike') etc and large quantities of nuclear bombs for strategic delivery, the USSR was far behind. The Soviet arsenal grew only later in size. This 'New Look' policy of the Eisenhower administration stressed the importance of technology over manpower.[46]

Massive Retaliation

The Korean War and the technological innovations had a far-reaching impact on the evolution of American national security doctrine. It was during this period that the Strategic Air Command (SAC), the Air Defence Command, and the nuclear

45. Morgan, n.6.
46. Jerome M *Kahan, Security in the Nuclear Age : Developing US Strategic Arms Policy* (Washington DC : Brookings Institution, 1975).

weapon's programme received top priority.[47] The Soviets had in the meantime demonstrated their non-nuclear capability.[48]

As a cheap alternative to conventional weapons, the strategy of 'Massive Retaliation' provided "more bang for the buck".[49] A direct product of the Korean War, it remained the official US strategy till 1961. The objective of massive retaliation was to instantly strike back where it hurt most by means and places of American choosing. It is not clear how large a conflict was envisaged to be countered by a massive retaliation. This uncertainty kept the rival wondering what response would result from a particular kind of attack. There were three occasions when the Eisenhower administration had to use the policy of massive retaliation to deal with Cold War challenges. The first occasion was in 1953, when Eisenhower sent a message of threat to Communist China that unless the stalled Korean truce negotiations bore fruit soon the US would use nuclear strikes on China. The Chinese accepted the UN armistice in a slightly modified form. The second opportunity arose when a veiled threat was communicated for a formal Armistice Day statement by Washington warning the Chinese

47. Partly influenced by the H-Bomb tested on August 8, 1953, Kalpan writes of the relief that the Americans felt because the Soviet H-Bomb was less powerful. However, while the US bomb was a device requiring refrigeration, which meant that the bomb could not be sent up on a rocket or a bomber, the Soviet fallout samples had lithium. This implied a quicker pace at which the Soviet ICBM was developing with the H-Bomb. Consequently, the US Atlas Project had to be pushed at a faster pace. See, Fred Kaplan, *The Wizards of Armageddon* (New York : Simon & Schuster, 1983), pp. 112-113.

48. Michael Howard, "Reassurance and Deterrence : Western Defence in the 1980's", *Foreign Affairs* (Winter 1982-83), p.310.

49. Charles Wilson quoted in B M Russett, "The Doctrine of Deterrence", in Philip J Murnion (ed), *Catholics and Nuclear War,* n. 34, p.152.

not to resume the war.[50] Finally, within a few months, the Chinese were threatened again of an attack if they intervened in the Vietnam War.

It is still unclear whether the Chinese needed to be deterred; it must also be noted that the Chinese were then a non-nuclear weapon state. As the Soviet nuclear arsenal grew, the American tendency to use nuclear threats declined but the Eisenhower administration did not give up the policy of massive retaliation. Another aspect of note is that it was as critics of the policy of massive retaliation that several civilian strategists published books and articles. This was the beginning of a new field of national security studies. Roots of the criticism lay in the potential for excessive violence and an attempt to find less dangerous ways to live with nuclear weapons. In the face of growing strategic power of the Soviet Union, there was less possibility of the US using the policy of massive retaliation.

This disbelief in the efficacy of the policy of massive retaliation was what really counted. The American commitment to NATO implied US acceptance to go for a nuclear war to defend Europe but the Europeans, especially the French, doubted this commitment. Secondly, massive retaliation was not exactly a rational rejoinder to a minor conflict.[51] Thirdly, it was feared that the policy made nuclear war more likely as the SAC bombers were concentrated in limited areas. Hence, even one Soviet bomber with nuclear bombs could destroy an entire base.[52] This could generate

50. The infamous massive retaliation speech by Dulles, was delivered in New York in January 12, 1954, while negotiation for a Korean cease-fire was in progress. Department of State Bulletin, 25 January 1954, pp. 107-110 in Graebner, *Ideas and Diplomacy : Readings in the Intellectual Tradition of American Foreign Policy* (New York : Oxford University Press, 1964), pp. 809-810 & in Catudal, n. 43, p. 106.
51. Lawrence Martin (ed), *Strategic Thought in the Nuclear Age* (Baltimore: John Hopkins University Press, 1979), pp. 4-15.
52. Richard K Betts, *Surprise Atta-k* (Washington DC : Brookings, 1982).

fear through uncertainty of a possible ground strike during a crisis and might pre-empt a nuclear first strike. By 1973, Kissinger asserted that once nuclear parity was achieved, a massive retaliation was nothing but "mutual suicide".[53]

Limited War

The Korean War had furthered strategic thinking on the concept of "Limited War." The war had been fought within a narrow belt although neither side was constrained by military, economic or technical reasons.[54] This system of "Graduated Deterrence" was debated heatedly in the 1950's as an alternative to an all out war.[55] As information on the growth of destructive capabilities and the after-effects of the fallout became available, the awareness about the gravity of the situation heightened.[56]

As there was no effective defence against the use of nuclear weapons, the imminence of a strategic stalemate was taken to be the best premise on which to base international relations. Bernard Brodie related the cause of military restraint to the universal fear of nuclear warfare. This, he hoped, would keep future wars between nuclear weapon states, or allied with those that have nuclear weapons, non-nuclear. He also assumed that limiting war in this way would become a general pattern.[57] Analysts believed that nuclear weapon states

53. Warner Levi, *The Coming End of War* (Beverley Hills, CA : Sage Publications, 1981), p.21.
54. Robert E Osgood, *Limited Nuclear War: The Challenge to American Strategic Policy* (Chicago : University of Chicago Press, 1957).
55. Bernard Brodle , "Unlimited Weapons and Limited War", *The Reporter,* Vol. II (1954), pp. 16-21. in Freedman, n.23.
56. "What mattered at the time were the variations in attitude over the use of nuclear weapons as instruments of international politics with the common consequence of destruction of the entire civilization." Refer to P M S Blackett, *Atomic Ways and the East-West Relations* (Cambridge: Cambridge University Press, 1956), p.3.
57. William Kaufmann, "The Crisis in Military Affairs", *World Politics,* Vol. 10, pp. 579-603.

would not resort to a nuclear attack as long as their objectives remained limited.

But the ability to keep a conflict limited due to the possibilities of escalation, was a matter of persistent anxiety.[58] Thomas Schelling finds the conception of limited war to be a method of tacit bargaining through escalation or limitation of conflict.[59] The threshold between nuclear and conventional weapons was never to be crossed as the guarantee that escalation could be avoided or even contained, was absent.[60] Diplomatic and political judgements had to transcend military factors. General Maxwell Taylor maintains that in order to avoid defeat in a limited war without resort to nuclear weapons, the US must opt for a sizeable conventional force.[61] But he is doubtful whether a war could be limited at all if nuclear weapons were used.

Tactical Nuclear Weapons

As an alternative to the limited war option and the option of having to maintain a large conventional army at all times, the Eisenhower administration came up with the idea of superiority and effectiveness of "tactical nuclear weapons" against enemy troops and any Korea-sized attack in the local war zone without having to expand the war geographically.[62] This theme of the British School of Graduated Deterrence was debated heatedly as an alternative to the threat of launching an all out nuclear war. In response to the superiority

58. William Kaufmann, "Limited Warfare", in Kaufmann (ed), *Military Strategy and National Security* (Princeton : Princeton University Press, 1956).
59. Thomas Schelling, *The Strategy of Conflict,* n.13.
60. Bernard Brodie, *Escalation and the Nuclear Option* (Princeton : Princeton University Press, 1966).
61. Maxwell Taylor, *The Uncertain Trumpet* (New York : Harper & Bros., 1959).
62. Robert E Osgood, *Limited Nuclear War,* n. 54.

of Soviet nuclear weapons, early limited war doctrine predicted the use of tactical nuclear weapons and the full use of strategic hydrogen bombs as a last resort. Proponents of Graduated Deterrence believed that such limited use of nuclear weapons could take place without triggering a full-scale strategic nuclear war between the contestants.[63] (The other option at that time, of course, was massive retaliation to handle limited wars that were expected to occur especially in the light of the Korean War experience.)

The prospect of total victory was replaced by reprieve from possible defeat. 'To stop when ahead but not victorious, or when behind but not defeated', was the political basis of the theory of Limited War. The hope was that once it was recognised that wars could be fought for limited ends, the problem of controlling a conflict would be more manageable. The policy depended on the superiority of US tactical nuclear weapons. Once the USSR had an equally large number of weapons, this policy became ineffective. Moreover, according to this policy, the US would have converted a conventional war into a nuclear war through the first use of tactical nuclear weapons. This, however, did not bother those who favoured Schelling's idea of viewing limited war as a tacit bargaining where each side bargained with the other about the ground rules, by deliberately escalating the conflict a bit but no more.[64] In principle, though limited war sought either on moral grounds or in terms of effective deterrence was preferred to an unlimited war, doubts were rampant on whether a limited war could in fact remain limited once tactical nuclear weapons were used. Thus, efforts to reduce the destructive effects of

63. This term originated with Hart and was prompted most vigorously by Rear Admiral Sir Anthony Buzzard, former Chief of British Naval Intelligence.
64. Thomas Schelling, *The Strategy of Conflict,* n.13.

a nuclear war through limitations on targets – counter-force rather than counter-value – were of not much use.

Liddell Hart, "the advocate of this logical control of war", sought to create awareness among people of the uselessness of war. Air power was seen as a source of escalation of conflicts through the bombing of civilians, thus, making a rational conduct of war more difficult. He further argued that with the advent of nuclear weapons future warfare would be subject to mutual restraints and certain agreed rules. Limited war also necessitated limited objectives.[65] Unfortunately, it was easier to limit wars in the past due to limitations of military technology than in the nuclear age.

It was suggested that the concept of limited nuclear war did not require large conventional forces.[66] The use of tactical nuclear weapons would strengthen both deterrence through denial and deterrence through punishment.[67] Denial capabilities, as Snyder has stated, worked by influencing the aggressor's estimate of his probability of gaining his objective, while punishment decided the estimate of possible costs and might have little effect on chances for territorial gains.[68] Thus, the Russian advance would be blocked and the process of blocking would be painful. The Russians would be punished.

The main proposition was that punishment should befit the crime and the need to concentrate on the military rather than the civilian targets. The counter-argument was that if the

65. Liddell Hart, *The Revolution in Warfare* (London: Faber & Faber, 1946), pp. 99-102.
66. B Brodie, "Unlimited Weapons and Limited War", *The Reporter* (November 1, 1954), in Freedman, n. 23.
67. To attack the Soviet Union or China. Read W Kaufmann, "The Crisis in Military Affairs", n. 57.
68. Glenn Snyder, *Deterrence and Defence,* n. 5.

intent was to punish, then the threat ought to be feared and certain to be implemented in the event of aggression. According to Peter Paret, "violence is the hallmark of any war, be it limited or extended. The only difference is that in a limited war, it does not require its fullest expression."[69]

However, there was an air of unreality about the whole effort to limit nuclear war. The very intention to go to war is not to set limits but to achieve the objectives at whatever cost. In fact, the best way to limit a modern war would be to avoid the use of nuclear weapons. Gradually Brodie, Blackett and Hart saw the idea of limited war as complicating the already confused situation without solving anything. The more the pressures built up against any use of nuclear weapons the greater the gap between deterrence policy, the military capability and psychological readiness.[70]

Confusion arose in the airmen's usage of the term 'strategic' to distinguish independent attacks on enemy's heartland in anticipation of decisive results from mere 'tactical' support of surface forces in the battle, which was considered a waste of air power. However, this differentiation between strategic and the tactical was merely semantic. Ultimately, the use of weapons requires decisions on targeting, avoidance of counter-measures and concentration on immediate objectives – the tactics. As some would say, there could never be a non-strategic or a non-tactical war.

Tactical counter-force warfare was viewed to be within the limits set by the Just War principle of *jus in bello*. But this does not necessarily make moral sense. Limitations were sought either on moral grounds or in terms of effective deterrence.

---

69. B Brodie, "More About Limited War", *World Politics*, October 10, 1957, p. 117. Also Hart, *Deterrence and Defence* (London : Stevens & Sons, 1960), p.81.
70. Henry Kissinger, "Conventional War : Limited or Nuclear? : A Reappraisal", *Daedalus*, Vol.89, No.4 (1960).

By using the adjective 'tactical' it was hoped to link nuclear weapons to the traditional land warfare. This link is illusory. Nuclear weapons cannot be considered just another weapon.[71] It was realised by the critics of this policy that delimiting weapons in advance would be of no advantage to the West and that a distinction between various types of weapons was not possible. Kissinger criticises the American way of thinking in terms of absolute values or objectives of total war-total victory. The gradual loss of technological superiority weakened the exploitation of this policy.

The prominent theorist Robert Osgood on the other hand has contended that "The detailed elaboration of strategic doctrine of limited war, the formulations, plans for carrying out this doctrine and the combined efforts of government, the military establishment, private analysts and publicists to translate the doctrine into particular weapons and forces are developed peculiar to the nuclear age."[72] Osgood justifies limited war as it maximises opportunity for effective use of military force as a rational instrument of policy. For a credible deterrence strategy the means of deterrence ought to be proportionate to the objective at stake.[73] This was the essential principle of the limited war theorists.

The American Catholic Bishops have rejected the concept of limited nuclear war as it might encourage the notion that nuclear war can be fought and won without transgressing moral limits. Limits could be discarded once a war is under way. They state thus, "The issue of Limited War is not simply the size of weapons contemplated or the strategies projected.

---

71. Freedman, n.23, p.119
72. R E Osgood, "The Reappraisal of Limited War" in ISS (Institute of Strategic Studies) *Problems of Modern Society* (UK: Chatto & Windus, 1970), pp. 93-95, at p. 94.
73. R E Osgood, *Limited Nuclear War*, n. 54, pp. 26 & 242.

The debate should include the psychological and political significance of crossing the boundary from the conventional to the nuclear arena in any form. To cross this divide is to enter a world where we have no experience of control, much testimony against its possibility and, therefore, no moral justification for submitting the human community to this risk. We, therefore, express our views that the first imperative is to prevent any use of nuclear weapons and our hope that leaders will resist the notion that nuclear conflict can be limited, contained or won in any traditional sense."[74]

They advocate a no first use policy. It is worthy of note that they realise the greater expense and delay in the development of an alternative by NATO. Ultimately, the Bishops attempt to abolish nuclear war and yet are left with no option but to suggest nuclear weapons as a deterer with use of nuclear weapons strictly forbidden. This is the same state of mind as existing till this day.[75]

Flexible Response

Determined to ensure non-use of nuclear weapons, the Kennedy-McNamara administration adopted the policy of Flexible Response. This theory of Maxwell Taylor maintained that nuclear weapons and the means for delivering them must be available at all times both for strategic war and for tactical use in local theatres. The objective was to deter all wars, general or limited, nuclear or conventional to convince all aggressors of the futility of attacking and to ensure the adequacy of bargaining power to give credibility to threat

74. "The Challenge of Peace : God's Promise and Our Response: The Pastoral Letter of The American Catholic Bishops – 1983," *Strategic Digest* (November 1983), pp. 691-745, at p. 717.
75. James Finn, "Pacifism & Just War : Either or Neither" in Philip J Murnion (ed.), *Catholics & Nuclear War,* n. 34, pp. 137-138.

and to achieve an end to arms race.[76] The idea was to deter the opponent from using his own nuclear forces of the same kind.[77]

Flexible response theorists believed that a stable deterrent balance was emerging between East and West vis-à-vis nuclear weapons for strategic and tactical use. It called for the US and its NATO allies to maintain sizeable conventional forces in being, at all times, which would make credible a policy decision to postpone early use of nuclear weapons.

With the Soviet Union catching up in nuclear arms development, deterrence became an even more "delicate balance of terror", at a time when mutual vulnerability was burgeoning.[78] The "controlled" US escalation of the conflict and the communist response raised the disturbing question: how could one indefinitely sustain such a strategy without greatly undermining not only the domestic economy but also the political consensus any government must have in order to function successfully. Those on the judgment-seat of flexible response sought to share the economic burden of Europe with European allies through maintenance of substantial armies in Europe.[79] They affirmed that having recovered from the ravages of the Second World War, the European allies could share the burden of military expenses. It was soon realised that the potential of the Red Army in Europe had been exaggerated. The divisions of the Soviet Armed Forces were smaller than their NATO counterparts.

76. Catudal, n.43, p. 113.
77. B Brodie, *Strategy in the Missile Age* (Princeton: Princeton University Press, 1959).
78. Albert Wohlstetter, "The Delicate Balance of Terror", *Foreign Affairs,* Vol. 37, No. 2 (January 1959), pp. 211-234. Provides an answer as to why second strike force is necessary for stable deterrence.
79. Jerome H Kahan, *Security in The Nuclear Age,* n. 46, esp. Chap. 4.

The total population of the NATO states was far larger than that of members of the Warsaw Pact.[80] It was also a matter of speculation whether the troops contributed by the East European states would participate wholeheartedly in a war engulfing the whole of Europe.

Flexible Response became the official NATO strategy in 1967. This was a strategy, which gave US the chance to use lower level options. There was no need to act quickly or in desperation. Deterrence threat would now be believed and thus would be effective; being effective, it would preserve the peace.[81]

The annotators of flexible response maintained that "the proposed buildup of NATO's conventional forces was totally beyond what the alliance would be willing to support." Still others argued that the dangers of limited use of nuclear weapons had been exaggerated. This strategy intended to deter an offensive by maintaining forces adequate to counter it at any level. The weakness of the policy was dramatically highlighted by US failure in Vietnam. The strategy "retained the ultimate escalatory threat of a strategic exchange between US and Soviet homelands to make clear the final magnitude of the dangers being contemplated." Albert Wohlstetter rightly placed his hand on the pulse of specialists' concern about the vulnerability of strategic forces, both, American and Soviet. According to him, stability is the greatest not when either side possessed greater advantage over the other but when both sides have relatively secure second-strike forces. Complete invulnerability to attack (the ideal case) was probably not to be hoped for. A constant and systematic campaign of deception too had to be avoided.

---

80. Andrew Cockburn, *The Soviet Threat : Inside The Soviet Military Machine* (New York : Random House, 1983), p. 104.
81. G Snyder, *Deterrence and Defence*, n. 5.

The strategy of flexible response encountered a number of problems. The most tenacious problem was the fact that the West Europeans were never quite convinced of its utility. These doubts were articulated by West European leaders especially General de Gaulle. The unwillingness of the Kennedy, and Johnson, administrations to contemplate use of nuclear weapons first, in defence of Europe, was espied as an indication of lack of a commitment to defend.

Flexible response demanded larger and better equipped Allied conventional forces in Europe.[82] As McNamara himself recalls, its "essential element", the development of "sufficient conventional capabilities to offset those of the Warsaw Pact" was never achieved. Moreover, the substantial raising of the nuclear threshold, envisioned when flexible response was first conceived, did not become a reality.[83] Both sides "virtually completely refurbished their inventories, increasing the number of weapons of all three different types – battlefield, intermediate-range and strategic..."

Assured Destruction

The capability of the US and the Soviet Union to harm each other in an equally decisive way created the predicament of "assured destruction."[84] Advanced by Secretary McNamara, the strategy had several engaging features. First, deterring through a secure second strike force would save on the expenses because America need not continuously strike for superiority against the Soviet Union. Second, the strategy had

82. Alain C Enthoven, "US Forces in Europe : How Many Doing What," *Foreign Affairs,* Vol. 53, No. 3 (April 1975), p. 518.
83. R S McNamara, "The Military Role of Nuclear Weapons : Perceptions and Misperceptions", *Foreign Affairs,* Vol. 62, No. 1 (Fall 1983), p. 65.
84. The term, "mutual assured destruction" was reportedly coined by Donald Brennan at the Hudson Institute. He disliked the idea of preserving peace through mutual vulnerability and coined the acronym MAD. In Catudal, n.43, p. 144.

the advantage of ruling out the use of nuclear arms as levers for political influence. Third, it would provide stimulus, to consider seriously any arms limitation agreements with the Soviet leadership.

For the critics, there was little evidence in this strategy to show that the Soviet Union subscribed to such a policy. It was militarily unacceptable and morally impossible. Fred Iklé questioned the morality of a strategy that would hold millions of civilians hostage to provocative acts of rivals over whom the Americans had no control.[85] There are also critics who have argued that the best way to deter Russians was to convince them of US's capability to win a nuclear war, at any level. With the signing of Anti Ballistic Missile Treaty in 1972, the US accepted the 'hostage' policy – a state of mutual vulnerability with the Soviet Union.

Assured destruction replaced the phase, of "assured retaliation". To the proponents of this strategy, its postulates were irrefutable. To critics, it was an antithesis of strategy – losing utility precisely when military strategy should come into effect – at the edge of war. Rather than minimising damage to the US and open avenues for an early settlement through further attacks, it had the sole aim of punishing aggression, which could lead to further counter attacks on the US, which a rational strategy would try to avoid.[86]

Criticising this policy, Richard Falk observes that the US nuclear weapon policy has been designed to translate nuclear

85. The master plan for US operations in a general nuclear war is called SIOP. Probably the most secret document in the Pentagon, it assigns nuclear weapons to specific targets under any given set of circumstances. Targeting plans are in the hands of Joint Chiefs of Staff. See Peter Pringle, et. al., *SIOP : The Secret US War Plan for Nuclear War* (New York : W.W. Norton, 1984).

86. Benjamin S Lambeth, *Selective Nuclear Options in American and Soviet Strategic Policy* (Santa Monica : RAND Corporation, 1976), p. 14.

offensive capability into political advantage.[87] Assured Destruction could determine the size and character of American strategic forces to measure their effectiveness. But the US had more weapons than required to carry out the assured destruction task. According to Lynn Davis, the actual war plans included large scale attacks against military targets (nuclear and conventional) and military plus urban industrial targets.[88]

Counter-force Strategy

The US forces were assigned on this mission against Soviet counter-force targets. The objective of the strategy was to make American commitment to its allies more credible and keep the US invulnerable.[89]

Secretary McNamara, first announcing this strategy publicly at the University of Michigan, Ann Arbor, in 1962 argued for a 'no cities' policy, early in the nuclear war (while reversing to the option if necessary) and giving the Soviets a powerful incentive not to attack US cities either.[90] This was a major shift from the 'city busting' emphasis of 1940's and 1950's.

The most convoluted aspect of this strategy was that this concept of damage limitation laid emphasis on first strike while the concept of "assured destruction" focussed on a strong and stable second strike, both leading to promotion of escalation. The former offensive and latter defensive avenues

---

87. R J Lifton, & Richard Falk, *Indefensible Weapons : The Political and Psychological Case Against Nuclearism* (New York : Basic Books, 1982), p. 175.
88. Lynn E Davis, *Limited Nuclear Options : Deterrence and The New American Doctrine* (London : Institute for Strategic Studies, 1975-76), p.1.
89. Roger D Speed, *Strategic Deterrence in the 1980's* (Palo Alto, California: Hoover Institution Press, 1979), p. 8. Making counter-force strikes, while holding back assured destruction forces was referred to as a "controlled response."
90. Desmond Ball, *Politics and Force Level : The Strategic Missile Programme of the Kennedy Administration* (Berkeley : University of California Press, 1980).

– the former coming handy as US had more strategic power than was required for "assured destruction".

Cuban Missile Crisis

Thus, a stalemate was created in the Cold War relations between the two super powers, caused unwittingly, by the mutual necessity to avoid a nuclear conflict. This stalemate was tested time and again during the Cold War by continuing technological competitions and by repeated crises of which the most intense was the Cuban missile crisis. The gradual and effective Soviet missile buildup seemed to make the security of the American deterrent more insecure.[91] History has recorded for posterity this crisis, which brought the world to the brink of a Third World War.

Had the Kennedy administration ordered a strike against missile sites in Cuba, the Russians could have retaliated by a counter-strike on the United States or on some vulnerable US missile located overseas. It could even have defied the US quarantine of Soviet missile carriers en route to Cuba. The Russian decision to respect the blockade (after 13 days of crisis)[92] was later said to be due to Western superiority and the Soviet fear of a nuclear war, not to forget the local and global support for US decisions. There were a few lessons learnt: such a crisis should not be escalated, and that the two sides should avoid the occurrence of another such situation. The nuclear stalemate became clear, politically and technologically.[93]

---

91. Alexander L George & R Smoke, *Deterrence in American Foreign Policy : Theory and Practice* (New York : Colombia University Press, 1974), esp. Chapter 15 & Ellie Abel, *The Missile Crisis* (Philadelphia : Lippincott, 1966), gives the best introduction to the crisis.
92. Robert S Kennedy, *Thirteen Days* (New York : Norton, 1969).
93. McGeorge Bundy, William J Crowe, Sydney D Drell, *Reducing Nuclear Danger : The Road Away From the Brink* (New York : Council on Foreign Relations Press, 1993), pp. 17-18.

2

Nuclear Deterrence and Nuclear Targeting

There are certain factors, which have influenced the development of nuclear strategy:-

a) Technological changes.

b) The work of strategic theorists.

c) The intelligence estimates, though accurate and timely, information was always lacking.

From 1945-1960, American nuclear strategy had progressed at three levels of government. The National Security Council with the President's approval defined the national security objective and promulgated the policy guidance. The President had the final authority regarding nuclear weapons. The military planners who attempted to translate high policy guidance into strategic plans and concepts. The two most directly concerned with nuclear conflict were the Joint Outline Emergency War Plan, which was changed to Joint Strategic Capability Plan (JSCP) in 1952 and the Joint Mid Range War Plan, which was changed to Joint Strategic Objective Plan in the same year. The Strategic Air Command (SAC) had the primary responsibility for operational planning to decide how best to employ available nuclear arsenal to achieve the objective contained in the JSCP.[1] SAC was both a separate, major, Air Force Command and a specified command within the Joint Chiefs of Staff (JCS) national unified command structure.

President Truman laid the foundation for the post War nuclear planning. The US Atomic Energy Commission was set up in 1946 to supervise the military and peaceful uses of atomic energy. The nuclear stockpile was initially very small. The secrecy was almost total. As late as February 1947, Secretary of the Navy and the Chief of Naval Operations each thought that the other knew the size of the nuclear stockpile when in fact neither had been told.[2] Not even President Truman was given the exact figures of the stockpile. His conception of the atomic bomb as an apocalyptic terror weapon of last resort compounded the secrecy. By setting up the AEC he sought to evade the military gaining control of the stockpile.

A lack of high level policy guidance plus extreme secrecy, slowed down any coordinated planning for nuclear war for two years after Hiroshima. The Joint Chiefs of Staff (JCS) did not approve any planning which contemplated the use of atomic bombs. The first atomic target list was prepared by war planners (generally on the use of atomic arsenal in a major confrontation with the USSR)[3] in the summer of 1947, incorporating it into the emergency war plan Broiler in the Fall of 1947. This plan selected 100 targets. The JCS war plans, the air offensive plans, Halfmoon and Frolic, emphasised an atomic air offensive. On July 28, 1948 the worsening Berlin crisis encouraged the Secretary of Defence James Forrestal to order the reconstitution

1. Robert D Lille, *Organizing for Strategic Planning ; The National System and the Air Force* (Washington DC. : USAF Historical Division Liaison Office, 1975).
2. David Allen Rosenberg, "US Nuclear Stockpile, 1945-1950", *The Bulletin of Atomic Scientists,* 38 (May 1982), pp. 25-30.
3. Ibid.

of planning for an atomic offensive.[4] Forrestal, Secretary of the Army Kenneth Royall and the Air Force leaders sought some definition of the circumstances that might justify an atomic war. The Air Force placed a paper before the National Security Council staff, discussing the possible repercussions of any policy statement on the use of atomic weapons. The NSC received it in September with two additions – the military must be ready to use:-

a) Appropriate means available including atomic weapons, in case of hostilities.

b) The decision to employ their use was assigned to the President.[5]

These additions were approved by the President on September 16, 1948 in NSC 30. That document remained the sole statement on American policy on atomic warfare approved by the NSC until 1960. Two pertinent questions were asked by the Air Force General Hoyt Vandenberg. What was the purpose to destroy the Russian people, industries, party hierarchy, or a combination of all ? Secondly, would the Americans occupy and reconstruct Russia or would they leave it to the Russians to work out their own salvation?[6]

The questions were addressed in part in the NSC 20/4 on November 23, 1948. It declared that in a general war it would seek to reduce or eliminate Soviet control inside and outside Soviet Union. There was no predetermined

4. D A Rosenberg, "American Atomic Strategy and the Hydrogen Bomb Decision", *The Journal of American History* 66 (June 1979), p. 79.

5. D A Rosenberg, "The Origins of Overkill ; Nuclear Weapons and American Strategy" in N Graebner (ed), *The National Security : The Theory and Practice, 1945-1960* (New York, 1986), p. 130. It was fortunate that I could go through this chapter as it provided me with all the knowledge that I required on targeting.

6. Ibid. It is indeed tough to find a better source than the works of Rosenberg. I have referred to his writings extensively in this chapter.

requirement for unconditional surrender established in it nor did it foresee the need to occupy the Soviet Union. This paper, aimed at total victory in a Russian-American conflict, was the last under the Truman administration. The burden of moral responsibility of using the bomb was left to the President. What was ignored was the increasing number of prospective Soviet targets, the growing complexity of atomic weapons and their delivery systems and the acquisition of atomic bombs by the Soviet Union.

Due to the absence of specific policy guidance, the most critical determinant in the strategic and operational planning was capability. During the periods of American nuclear monopoly (1945-1948) the stockpile and delivery capability remained limited. At the end of 1945, there were only 2 weapons in the stockpile, 9 in July 1946; 13 in July 1947 and 50 in July 1948 and none of them were assembled. They were all Mark 3 "Fat Man" implosion bombs weighing 10,000 pounds each, were inefficient in their use of fissionable material and took 39 men over two days to assemble. To load these weapons into the bombers, a special hoist in a deep pit was required. There were only some 30 B-29s in the SAC, modified to drop the atomic bombs. Prior to the advent of the aircraft (U-2), and reconnaissance and satellite capabilities (SAMOS, Corona), there was no way an attack could differentiate between military assets and civilian areas.[7] By the fall of 1947, 100 urban centres for an atomic attack had been identified. By 1949, Soviet government control centres and urban industrial concentrations became the target. SAC, unable to even maintain this distinction, gave priority to the annihilation of population, industrial locations being treated as incidental targets.[8]

7. John Prados, *The Soviet Estimate: U.S. Intelligence Analysis and Russian Military Strength* (New York: Dial Press, 1982).
8. Rosenberg, n. 5, p. 132.

Plans for an air offensive against Russian targets increased with the nuclear stockpile. The war plan Broiler called for 34 bombs on 24 cities. The Air Force Harrow war plan, which served to support JCS war plan Frolic and Halfmoon, contemplated 50 bombs on 20 Soviet cities. Joint war plan Trojan, approved in December 1948, called for attack on 70 cities with 133 atom bombs. In May 1949, Lieutenant General H R Harmon, reported to the JCS that even if all 133 bombs detonated with precision, this would neither bring capitulation, nor destroy communism or destroy the Soviet leadership. The air offensive would in fact produce reactions detrimental to the achievement of the allied war objectives.[9] The Harmon Committee, set up by the Secretary of Defence James Forrestal to evaluate the impact of the atomic air offensive against the Soviet Union, sought to assuage the Soviet phobia that persisted then. The report went on to state that the industrial capacity of the Soviet Union and the rapid advance of the Soviet forces into selected areas of Western Europe and the Middle and Far East would not be totally impaired as expected. This was the announcement that led to the evolution of the strategy of Dropshot that paved the way for passing importance to other targets rather than population and industry.

The October 1949 target annex for Joint Outline Emergency War Plan Offtackle called for attack on 104 urban targets with 220 atomic bombs plus a re-attack reserve of 72 nuclear weapons. The only retardation targets were the petroleum refineries, electric power plants, submarine yards and synthetic ammonia plants, some of them in Eastern Europe. The aim, as the Dropshot requirement study stated, was to destroy the will of the enemy "through selective attack of limited complexes or mass attack of people."[10] The plan required 300 atom bombs

9. Rosenberg, n. 5, pp. 68-71.
10. Anthony Cane Brown (ed), *DROPSHOT: The American Plan for World War II Against Russia in 1957* (New York: Dial Press, 1978).

and 20,000 tons of high explosive conventional bombs on about 700 targets, located in approximately 100 urban areas.[11] In all this, the prior approval of the President was required. The aim was total victory and the option of unconditional surrender was ignored. These objectives, mentioned in the NSC-30, remained the sole statement on American foreign policy, till 1960, on atomic warfare.

The third targeting category soon appeared on August 15, 1950, in the midst of the ongoing conflict in Korea. The JCS formally assigned 'first priority' to the destruction of known targets affecting Soviet capabilities. Second priority was assigned to the retardation mission and 'third priority' to attack on Soviet liquid fuel, electric power and the atomic energy industries.[12] These categories were code-named Bravo, Romeo and Delta. With the broadening of the industrial targets, targets category and other changes, they formed the basic framework for US nuclear targeting for a decade.[13]

Bernard Brodie, then a Yale University Professor, criticised the target list in December 1950. According to him, there was no calculated strategy for destroying the Soviet capacity to make war. General Curtis LeMay emphasised the need to target industries located in urban areas, so that even if a bomb missed its target, a "bonus" could be derived from its use. This, according to him, would conserve the nuclear stockpile while SAC could inflict maximum damage on the Soviet Union's war-making capacity. Brodie characterised these targeting schemes as

---

11. Ibid., p.23.
12. D A Rosenberg, n.5.
13. Bernard Brodie, *War and Politics* (New York : Macmillan, 1973), p.64, in Rosenberg, n.5., p.133.

"sheer frivolousness and stupidity with respect to the number one strategic problem confronting the US at the time."[14]

In October 1948, when General LeMay assumed command of the SAC, there was a lack of operational readiness. He initiated the task of building a mobile operational force. He undertook a crash programme to build SAC into a "cocked weapon" to deliver at least 80% of its atomic stockpile simultaneously.[15] Its nuclear capable aircraft increased from 60 in December 1948 to 250 by June 1950. By 1952, SAC was training in earnest for its blunting mission, and its intelligence gathering improved with SAC RB-36 and RB-50 aircraft flying electronic and photo reconnaissance missions. However, only a few crossed Soviet borders. In fact, between 1949 and 1953, the bulk of intelligence on the USSR came from Project Wringer.

Interestingly, the increasing importance of the SAC was due to the role of the Air Force in the strategic targeting of Germany and Japan during the Second World War. They also feared, quite unnecessarily, that the Navy and its aviators were attempting to take over the strategic bombing mission. Once Truman reluctantly accepted nuclear weapons as the centre-piece of American Armed Forces, the NSC 68/4, in December 1950, went ahead for a phased and balanced build up of American armed forces through June 1952. The forceful arguments of the Air Force Secretary Thomas K Finletter and Chief of Air Staff, Vandenberg, in favour of the utility of adequate delivery capabilities to transport the expanding nuclear production, made the JCS assign primacy to the Air Force and the buildup of SAC. The Fiscal Year 1953

14. Walter S Poole, *The History of Joint Chiefs of Staff and National Policy*, Vol. 1, 1945-47; Vol. 2, 1947-49; vol.4, 1950-51, (Wilmington, Del: Michael Glagier, 1977, 1980), pp. 165-167.
15. n.5, p.136.

budget manifested the Air Force objective for June 1954 of 143 wings, there were to be 48 more than proposed in NSC 68/4. The ever-increasing target estimates shaped the growth of the nuclear stockpile; the stockpile itself galvanised the expansion of SAC. In January 1952, Truman approved a 50% increase in plutonium and a 150% increase in enriched uranium as according to Vandenberg, there seemed to be "perhaps 5-6000 Soviet targets which would have to be destroyed in the event of war." Labelled as "boot strapping", the Air Force generated target lists justified the weapons production, which in turn justified the increased appropriation to provide matching delivery capabilities.

As intelligence improved, the Air Force target list surpassed the growth of the stockpile. By January 1953, there were 8 plutonium production reactors in place of 5 and 10 gaseous diffusion plants in place of 2. The stockpile of approximately 1000 weapons in the summer of 1953, grew to nearly 18000 by the end of the decade.[16] These were more powerful and sophisticated. The 20 KT yield of a Mark 3 bomb multiplied more than 25 times between 1948-52.

There were advances in the design, composition, stability and power of the high explosives used to detonate a fission core, as well as a betterment in the mechanical structure and composition of the fissile pit itself. This effected higher yields and increased efficiency in the use of fissionable material, permitting the November 1952 test of Mark 18 Super Orally (U 235) bomb, which yielded 500 KT.[17] The new "boosted" weapons, which

16. William M Arkin, Thomas B Cochran, & Milton M. Hoenig, "The US Nuclear Stockpile," *Arms Control Today*, 12 (April 1982), pp. 1-2. Richard G Hewlett, & Francis Duncan, *History of the United States Atomic Energy Commission*, Vol. II : Atomic Shield, 1947-1952 (University Park : Pennsylvania State University Press, 1969), p. 169, in n.1.

17. Rosenberg, n. 2, pp. 27-28.

was first tested in April 1951, employed a small amount of fusion fuel within a "hollow implosion" core. This was done to further increase the efficiency and yield of nearly one megaton. In October 1952, the US fired the first true thermonuclear weapon.

By the time Truman left office in January 1953, the framework for nuclear strategy had emerged and the era of nuclear plenty was launched. American war planning was conducted with an incomparable intensity during peacetime. A "new family" of war plans on the authority of the Joint Chiefs of Staff was created :-

a) The Joint Strategic Capability Plan (JSCP) was created to deal with the military situation as in the year of formation.
b) Joint Strategic Objective Plan (JSOP), which established force and mobilisation requirements for the next three to five years.
c) Joint Long Range Strategic Estimate (JLRSE) to guide research and development.

Contrary to Truman's belief that a preventive atomic war was irrational and that there was a need for civilian control over these weapons, within six months of assuming office Eisenhower transferred a sizeable number of atomic weapons to the military for deployment to specific bases afloat and ashore.[18] This was to reduce the vulnerability of the stockpile and to increase its operational readiness. Contrary to Truman's view of these weapons as weapons of last resort, for Eisenhower they were weapons of first-use. A high level review of policy options of containment, spheres of influence and roll-back code named Operation Solarium, was undertaken. On October 30, 1953, Eisenhower approved NSC 162/2 as the basic national policy. This was the first statement of national policy to address the issue of tactical

18. Rosenberg, n. 5, p. 141.

nuclear weapons directly. It sanctioned the use of nuclear weapons as any other munitions. The defence programme in 1953 outlined for the first time the provision for tactical atomic support for US and allied military forces.

The move towards the development of an effective system of continental defence was accelerated when in July 1953, Soviet Union tested a 300-400 KT fission weapon and announced its thermonuclear capability which might force US to initiate a war in self defence. In August 1953, an Air Force study entitled "The Coming of National Crisis" stated that in the following years the US would find itself in a militarily unmanageable position. It maintained that soon it would have to choose between trusting its future to the "whims of a small group of proven barbarians" in the Soviet Union or be militarily prepared to support decisions, which might involve a general war.[19]

The new strategy required not only defence against local aggression but also massive retaliation, striking power and tactical nuclear weapons. Project Vista, a study undertaken for use of a specific number of atomic bombs by the Navy and 'soon-to-be-deployed' Air Force tactical air units, concluded that the tactical employment of atomic weapons was essential for defending West Europe and that a strategic offensive be withheld for humanitarian, political and military reasons.

Tactical nuclear weapons were weapons of first strike and deployed in the forward positions overseas – more dangerous than the strategic weapons deployed in silos and in submarines. Not only are these weapons vulnerable in case of local wars and revolutions, they are also exposed in the event the policy of first use is abandoned. These weapons,

---

19. Glenn Snyder, "The New Look of 1953," in Warner Schilling, et.al., *Strategy, Politics and Defence Budgets* (New York: Columbia University Press, 1962), pp. 379-524.

promoted by Robert Oppenheimer in his discussions with President Eisenhower, were incorporated in the Project Vista. The enduring example of his persuasive power is the incorporation of 6000 of these tactical nuclear weapons in NATO, Europe. The design behind this tenacity is equally important to be noted. Oppenheimer feared the spread of Korean War to Europe. He also feared that a local invasion of West Berlin or West Germany would be responded with the Air Force plans of 1952. The US, after all, had a substantial advantage over the Soviet nuclear forces – quantity-wise and in means of delivery. The Soviets would, of course, counteract by attacking Paris or London, if their surviving nuclear weapons cannot reach the US after a tactical nuclear attack. Tactical nuclear weapons were, thus, to act as a counterweight to the Soviet tank armies and to the Strategic Air Command (SAC). Moreover, Truman did not want the military to gain control of the nuclear stockpile. It was Eisenhower who transferred a sizeable number of atom bombs to the military to deploy them. By 1953, SAC had identified 409 airfields from which the Soviet Union could launch nuclear strikes. In March 1954, SAC's Basic War Plan called for up to 735 bombers to hit Soviet early warning screens from all directions, simultaneously using chaff and other electronic countermeasures to overwhelm the Soviet defences. This would minimise the time the American bombers would remain in hostile air space, maximise destruction and reduce the need for costly follow-up strikes.

In July 1953, the Soviets tested the fission weapons of 300-400KT. In October 1953, the JCS Chairman, Arthur Radford, urged a 'graduated use of nuclear weapons'. Priority was given to the destruction of military forces operating against the US and its allies and the facilities, which supported them before the launching of unrestricted retaliatory operations.[20]

The expansion of the Soviet nuclear arsenal forced the Eisenhower administration to re-evaluate its defence strategy. The Technological Capabilities Panel (TCP) chaired by the President of MIT, James R Killian Jr, submitted in February 1955 a report entitled "Meeting the Threat of Surprise Attack." It predicted the expansion of threat as Soviet acquired true thermonuclear weapons and long-range delivery aircraft. The report observed that the US could maintain strategic superiority for three to five years but would be vulnerable to a devastating surprise attack. Priority was attached to improved intelligence, tactical warning capabilities and the preparation for instantaneous response, including the use of nuclear-armed air defence missiles. It recommended the grant of "advance authority for instant use of the atomic warheads wherever needed over the land areas of the US and Canada" and the dispersion of nuclear weapons to offensive and defensive forces. The report reaffirmed the Bravo, Romeo and Delta targeting priorities while stressing the inter-relationship between the offensive and defensive forces. It also anticipated a period of instability for the US in the late 1950s once the advantage would rest with that side which acquired ballistic missiles in large numbers. This concern prompted the NSC to adopt a flexible military plan emphasising the importance of containing limited conflicts.

The Weapons Systems Evaluation Group (WSEG-12) submitted a report and predicted in February 1955 that the

---

20. George F Lemmer, *The Air Force and Strategic Deterrence : 1951 - 1960* (Washington DC. : Office of Air Force History, 1980) and Rosenberg, "A Smoking Radiating Ruin at the End of Two Hours, Document of American Plans for Nuclear War with the Soviet Union: 1954-55", *International Security* 6 (Winter 1981-82), pp. 3-38.

atomic offensive could achieve the ultimate goal of ending a general war in a single blow. It would destroy all Soviet atomic production capabilities, obliterate 118 out of 184 major cities, cause 60 million deaths, eliminate Soviet bloc industrial capabilities and destroy any chance of recuperation for at least a year. However, even if SAC destroyed 645 targeted airfields, around 240 would nevertheless survive. To destroy all Soviet airfields, one would require twice the number of weapons allocated and hit first to avoid a Soviet first-strike.[21]

In May 1955, a National Intelligence Estimate (NIE) estimated that the Soviet Union had some 20 "Bear" turbo-prop and 20 "Bison" jet heavy long-range bombers. Much more disquieting was the prognostication that the Soviets would have approximately 700 heavy bombers by mid-1959, as well as 700 "Badgers". The advances in weapons technology merely complemented the expanding Soviet delivery capability. In November 1955, a 1.6-megaton test confirmed the accomplishment of a true two-stage thermonuclear capability by the Soviet Union.[22] The possession of such weapons by the USSR could seriously damage the US even if only a few bombers manage to penetrate the American defence. The "bomber gap" represented a serious threat to the country's ability to disarm an impending Soviet strike.

In mid-January 1956, Eisenhower gave expression to the appalling "chaos and destruction" the US would suffer in a thermonuclear war and urged the NSC to continue to maintain a five-year strategic materials stockpile, believing that it was

---

21. Ibid., pp. 29-38 & John Ponturo, *Analytical Support for the Joint Chiefs of Staff : The WSEG Experience, 1948-1976* (Arlington, VA : Institute for Defence Analysis Study, S-507, July 1979), p. 101.
22. D Holloway, "Soviet Thermonuclear Development", *International Security* 4 (Winter 1979-80) pp. 192-197.

"crazy" to think that any war could be "won or lost" in a period of thirty days. Yet, he asked his strategists to consider seriously the consequences "if we reach a point where we will have passed the limits of what human beings can endure."

On March 15, 1956, the NSC adopted flexible military plans and emphasised "the importance of containing limited conflicts. The NSC 5602/1 maintained use of nuclear weapons in military operations short of general war as authorised by the President. It rejected preventive war but affirmed the national determination to prevail in a general war." Most significantly, it anticipated the need for pre-authorisation for the use of nuclear weapons.

In 1956, the Air Force began to address the problem of bomber force vulnerability and the need to recognise the drastically reduced tactical warning time. The RAND analysts recommended improvements in Early Warning Systems and SAC response time, dispersal of the bomber force, and more effective airfield defences. In response, the SAC moved to construct or acquire additional bases in the United States and Canada. It conducted a series of tests from November 1956 through September 1957 to evaluate the human and material requirements of holding one-third of the bomber force on fifteen-minute ground alert.[23]

The Gaither Committee Report entitled "Deterrence and Survival in the Nuclear Age", declared only moderate support for fallout shelters, and instead assigned highest priority to the improvement of SAC survivability. The report stated the country's requirement of an effective deterrent in the form of secure and effective retaliatory striking force, as "by 1959

23. Staff Report "Protecting United States Power to Strike Back in the 1950s and 1960s" (Santa Monica : Rand Corporation Report R-290, Contract No. AF-18 (600-1600), September 1, 1956).

the USSR may be able to launch an attack with ICBMs carrying megaton warheads against which SAC will be almost completely vulnerable under the present program." It urged acceleration of the ballistic missile programmes, with particular emphasis on the Polaris submarine launched IRBM because of its advantages of mobility and reduced vulnerability. Three committee members, the President was informed privately, had advocated the reconsideration of the option of preventive war as a means of avoiding a situation of extreme peril.[24]

Despite its political volatility, the Gaither Report was more a symptom than a cause of change. Eisenhower believed that the United States was facing a gradual deterioration of strategic advantage, not an immediate crisis. The man who had dispelled the 'missile gap' with a nonchalant wave of the hand, Eisenhower now authorised immediate nuclear response for an assortment of emergency conditions. Thus, by 1958, the SAC was authorised to implement a 'fail safe' rapid response 'without the risk of nuclear war through miscalculation'. Despite Eisenhower's efforts to dispel it, this "missile gap" became an exploitable political issue for democratic presidential hopefuls and would not prove to be an illusion until the first Discover and Samos satellites documented the miniscule size of the Soviet missile capability in 1960-61.[25]

Eisenhower's approach to protecting US bombers in the missile age was not to increase their survivability on the ground, but to ensure that they would be in the air at the time of any surprise attack. The government did not implement the programme of bomber-blast shelters recommended by the Gaither Committee. On the other hand it made a concerted

24. Lille, n. 1 and Rosenberg, n.5.
25. John Prados, n.7.

effort to increase tactical warning time and rapid response. In January 1958, Defence Secretary Neil McElroy authorised the development of the Ballistic Missile Early Warning System (BMEWS) to complement the Distant Early Warning Line that was activated in August 1957. To reduce the reaction time further, on May 22, 1957 Eisenhower issued an authorisation for the employment of nuclear weapons, which gave permission for an immediate nuclear response under a variety of emergency conditions. It was realised that so complex were the instructions needed to implement this authorisation that the Departments of Defence and State did not approve it until February 17, 1959. Finally, in late 1960, each of the unified and specified commanders received a series of still classified directives regarding the immediate use of nuclear weapons.

In 1959, SAC achieved its goal of holding one-third of the bomber force on ground alert. In March 1958, the Chief of Staff of the Air Force authorised SAC to implement the "fail safe" or "positive control" system, which would permit rapid response without the risk of initiating war through miscalculation. In 1959, the SAC plan to establish an airborne alert, consisting of one-fourth of the B-52 force, was approved by the JCS. However, due to the sizeable cost of incessant operations it was recommended that the plan be put into operation only when the President considered such a special caution essential.[26] The advances in weapons design facilitated to a great extent the development of SAC alert plans. The SAC's delivery capability continued to expand. At its peak in 1959, SAC had nearly 500 B-52s, more than 2000 B-47s and over 1000 propeller and jet driven tanker aircraft; the

26. Robert F Futrell, *Ideas, Concepts, Doctrine : A History of Basic Thinking in the US Air Force : 1907-1964, Vol 11* (2 volumes), (Maxwell Air Force Base, Ala : Aerospace Studies Institute, 1971), pp. 578-582.

supersonic B-58 would enter service in August 1960. This growth in the bomber force remained linked to expanding target lists, which totalled 2,997 in 1956, and 3,261in early 1957. By the end of the decade, SAC had analysed over 20,000 potential Soviet-bloc targets, grouping the most important of these into Desired Ground Zeros (DGZs) consistent with the blast radii of large yield thermonuclear weapons. Expansion of the list resulted largely due to the identification of additional "counterforce" targets, especially airfields and suspected missile sites, and due to the poor quality of target intelligence that galvanised 'decorative' guesswork.

In the Spring of 1957, Army Chief of Staff, Taylor and Chief of Naval Operations, Arleigh Burke instructed their staffs to prepare a joint analysis of high yield weapons requirements, focussing on the radiation and fallout that would follow any implementation of the SAC war plan. On August 28, 1957, the hastily prepared but devastating critique – Project Budapest, reached the JCS. It demonstrated that far more weapons were being assigned to targets than were required to realise the damage required by the JSCP, and that the resulting radiation and fallout would be dangerously and unnecessarily high. There were as many as 17 overlaps on a single location. Additional and duplicate weapons had been assigned in profusion, even when the supplemented damage they would achieve was minimal. Air Force leaders, including Nathan Twining, who had become JCS Chairman, Air Force Chief of Staff, Thomas White and the new Air Force Vice Chief Curtis LeMay, were incensed by this indictment. Every additional gallon of fuel oil destroyed, he declared, could otherwise help carry another Russian bomber towards the United States.[27]

27. n.5, p.160.

The JSCP guidance regarding nuclear targeting was only applicable to the situations in which general war began gradually or with enough strategic warning to permit SAC to launch its strike force before the Soviet attack arrived. The US needed stand-in guidance to 'provide for the possibility of a general war initiated under disadvantageous conditions'. The alternative planning required that each unified and specified commander "select from his target list those high priority targets, which would be attacked if only 25% of his atomic delivery forces would be available for employment." Infinitesimal number of weapons would be assigned to achieve at least a moderate damage to each target ensuring maximum utilisation of the depleted resources. "SAC would target the Soviet nuclear delivery capability only to the extent where it would be profitable on the assumption that much of the capability would have been expanded." This course was to augment the existing target lists. The plan would be implemented on the assurance that the American forces had been depleted enough to make 'primary undertaking' impossible.The policy injected into the JCS guidance, for the first time, the concept of a strictly retaliatory nuclear strategy, which would necessitate the preparation of a high priority target list. This scheme for an alternative undertaking was approved by the JCS in early 1958. However, the putting in order of the new target list progressed slowly.

The efforts of the Army and the Navy to place limits on the strategic offensive reflected their concern about the US requiring improved capabilities for a limited conflict. Secretary of State Dulles emphasised the need to prepare for local conflicts. Eisenhower believed that an increased conventional force would result in the increased defence spending or reduced strategic forces, the former resulting in the formation of a garrison state.[28] His policy of minimum force requirements became the American policy in 1959. Targeting an industrial military combination with emphasis on urban-industrial areas would require fewer weapons and their delivery systems. He had begun to question the effectiveness of maintaining an entirely counter-force capability. However, he was critical of the military requirements, which had reached the level of capability to destroy "every conceivable target all over the world" and had a reserve three times more than what was required. The JCS believed that 70 targets would be enough to defeat the Soviet Union. An adequate minimum striking force was as yet unclear. A new approach was worked out with three alternate target systems:-

a) Primarily military.

b) Primarily urban-industrial (as proposed by the Army and the Navy).

c) A mix of the two.

This was analysed on the basis of not just deterring a war but with the object of 'prevailing' in a general war. This policy embodied the assumption that there was no link between deterrence and target selection as deterrence depended on Soviet perceptions and they were not privy to the American target list.[29]

In July 1958, Admiral Burke laid out the basic elements of his concept of "finite deterrence" as an all out war was no more valid due to the deployment of the Soviet ICBM force in unknown sites, rendering it impossible for the Americans to disarm the Soviets. A mobile and concealed

---

28. General Maxwell D Taylor, *The Uncertain Trumpet* (New York ; Harper & Row, 1959), pp. 57-65.
29. n.5, p. 164.

force, according to Burke, would be effective. This would provide the American security strategists the necessary time to think without the pressures for a first strike. The US could choose to respond gradually while trying to apply political coercion. This would require a modest force – just enough for deterrence (ie for an ability to destroy major urban areas), and the US would be in a position to achieve a thermonuclear stalemate. All this is stated to have been brought about by the Navy in order to exploit the flexibility and invulnerability of the Polaris submarines.

By the summer of 1959, the Navy strategists had further refined finite deterrence. The most effective retaliatory targeting system would be political and military command and control centres and critical industries. The Navy projected a fleet of 45 submarines, 29 deployed all the time, capable of destroying 232 targets. The total costs would be 7 to 8 billion. Budget Director Maurice Stans raised the very appropriate question of the utility of having "other IRBMs or ICBMs, SAC aircraft and overseas bases." The policy of finite deterrence, and the importance attached to Polaris replacing SAC, was a serious challenge to the Air Force.

Unable to fault the Polaris technically, the Air Force prepared a systematic defence of the counter-force targeting. Finite deterrence was regarded as incapable of discouraging limited Soviet strikes. The US required forces adequate to maintain the initiative under all circumstances of war. In May 1959, General White approved an estimate of future force objectives necessary to implement the Air Force strategy. It predicted that by 1963, some 8400 Soviet targets would require destruction and by 1970, 10,000. Since multiple weapons would be assigned to each DGZs to achieve 90% destruction specified in Air Force war plans, the US would require by 1968 a force of 3000 Minuteman, 150 Atlas and 110 Titan ICBMs and a combined total of nearly 900 B-52, B-58 and B-70 and nuclear powered bombers.

RAND analysts Herbert Goldhammer and Andrew Marshall further supported the argument against a counter-population strategy by stating that "there are few things so bad that not thinking about them won't make them worse." A strike on civilians could be taken as a symbol of weakness. They proposed a strategy of "partial withholding", launching only a portion of surviving SAC forces against selected targets while threatening destruction of Soviet cities unless they agreed to American terms. This would have the advantage of extending the pre-war deterrence threat into the intra-war period and might terminate the nuclear exchange.[30]

In March 1960, the Air Force Intelligence Directorate completed a detailed analysis of targeting requirements. The target planners estimated that there would be a total of 3560 targets in 1960, 6300 in 1965 and 6955 in 1970, reflecting an increase in Soviet missile sites. The Air Force rejected the argument of the Army and the Navy of deterrence as the sole objective, and that counter-force had become too expensive in the missile age.

There was also the problem of reviewing target lists and war plans for inconsistencies and duplication. Out of 2400 targets, there were 300 duplications, which could have resulted in the destruction of friendly aircraft in chaotic wartime conditions. A report prepared in 1960 recommended a target list for 1962 Fiscal Year consisting of 2021 targets, including 120 ICBM sites, 140 air defence bases, 200 bomber bases, 218 military and government control centres, 124 other military targets – naval bases, nuclear weapons facilities – with the remaining targets located within 131 urban centres. It

30. Herbert Goldhammer, & Andrew W Marshall, with the assistance of Nathan Leites, *The Deterrence and Strategy of Total War, 1959-1961: A Method of Analysis* (RAND Corporation : RM 2301, April 30, 1959), p. 131.

rejected non-city counter-force and finite deterrence and opted for combining a decisive blow with a blunting attack on Soviet nuclear delivery capability.[31] By late 1959, Eisenhower's concept of Massive Retaliation had been reduced to a strategy of desperate resolve. Eisenhower held the belief that the US must have the ability to destroy anyone who strikes first "because the biggest thing today is to provide a deterrent to war."[32] Meanwhile, he had ruled out making a full commitment to the Polaris programme till it was fully tested. The Eisenhower administration's top secret review of "US Policy in the Event of War", approved by the NSC in March 1959, retained the option of pre-emptive response to an impending Soviet strike without specifically endorsing it.

On July 6, 1960 Secretary of Defence, Gates reported to the President that in fifteen meetings with the JCS since taking office in January, he had been unable to resolve the basic disagreements over targeting and coordination. On August 11, 1960, Eisenhower approved the creation of the Joint Strategic Target Planning Staff (JSTPS) under SAC to prepare the National Strategic Target List and the Single Integrated Operational Plan (SIOP). On 27 November, Eisenhower received Burke's memorandum and was shocked by the level of overkill that had been achieved. The high assurance criteria had been negated.

Although SACs commitment to maximise the impact of available forces accounted for the level of overkill, it was the emphasis on the need for plenty of nuclear weapons and its delivery vehicles that made such a move possible. Both, Truman and Eisenhower administrations promoted the expansion of the strategic striking force. The overlapping and

---

31. n.5, p.170.
32. Ibid

duplication that accompanied the induction of missiles in lieu of bombers, in fact, worsened the situation. On December 2, 1960, the JCS approved SIOP-62. At the time of Eisenhower leaving office, SAC had 538 B-52, 1,292 B-47 and 19 B-58 bombers and 1,094 tankers. The US had deployed 12 Atlas ICBMs and 60 Thor IRBMs in Britain. It was deploying 30 Jupiter IRBMs in Italy and had agreed to deploy them in Turkey as well. Over 650 Atlas, Minuteman and Titan missiles were under contract as were 14 Polaris submarines carrying 16 missiles each. The first Polaris submarine *USS George Washington* departed on deterrent patrol in November 1960.[33]

Eisenhower remained committed to tactical nuclear weapons in limited conflict situations, though he doubted if a war could ever be limited once nuclear weapons were used. Between 1958-1960, the stockpile of tactical nuclear weapons swelled from 6,000 to 18,000. When he left office, SAC had trained and prepared for massive retaliation and massive pre-emption for a decade. Gross overestimation of Soviet nuclear forces due to inadequate intelligence was also one of the factors that contributed to the unnecessary expansion of US forces. Despite such increase in weapons, the ability to disarm the Soviet Union seemed to be unrealisable.

The Kennedy Period

With the coming of the Kennedy administration, Secretary of Defence Robert McNamara, disturbed by the rigidity of defence planning and the absence of a clear and lucid strategic rationale for the urban industrial target mix and counter-force, initiated a re-evaluation of the American strategic posture. He incorporated second-strike counter-force and the partial withholding of strategy,[34] which RAND analysts had advocated.

---

33. Desmond Ball, *Politics and Force Levels : The Strategic Missile Program and the Kennedy Administration* (Berkeley : University of California Press, 1980), pp. 31-34.
34. Ibid., pp.119-120 & 186-190.

McNamara believed that a nation must respond to surprise attacks first by striking Soviet bomber bases, missile sites and other installations dealing with long-range nuclear forces. This would limit the damage done to the US by Soviet follow-on forces, while still holding in reserve, forces that could destroy Soviet urban society.

To adapt the SIOP to the new strategic posture, new directives of 1961, for SIOP 63 mandated the separation of the optimum mix target system into its major components. The new targeting categories were: Soviet strategic nuclear capability, other nuclear capability (nuclear command installations) and the urban industrial base. These were the reformed versions of Bravo, Romeo and Delta, established in 1950. Plans were to withhold attacks against one or more of these targets and against China and the satellite nations. These plans followed a series of pre-emptive and retaliatory options that were designed to permit flexibility in response to varied political and military conditions.[35] Despite these restraints there was a continued upswing on force developments. SIOP continued to emphasise capabilities rather than the objectives, giving accent to the fact that never fewer than "thousands of weapons" be applied to areas targeted.[36] For more than two decades, SIOP dominated the US thinking about nuclear war. "You very seldom see a cowboy", Arleigh Burke has aptly remarked, "even in the movies, wearing three guns. Two is enough."[37]

The Nixon Administration: From 'Superiority' to 'Sufficiency'

Accepting McNamara's idea of desirability of 'parity' or rough equivalence with the USSR in strategic forces, the

35. Ibid, p.190-192.
36. Futrell, n. 26, pp.622-27.
37. Remark made at Kissinger's seminer at Harvard, in Spring 1960, quoted in n.5, p.178.

principle of "sufficiency" became the watchword of the Nixon administration. The problem was, as John L Gaddis explained, "objectives tended to expand as means did, thereby producing not only eventual exhaustion but also increasing resistance from other nations."[38] Economic necessity had led the Johnson administration to the same conclusion and wisdom was "elevated to the status of doctrine."[39]

However, Nixon discovered that the administration had inherited a much larger strategic nuclear force than was needed to destroy Soviet (and even Chinese) cities. The long-range missiles equipped with 5,300 warheads, each of which could be targeted separately went to station around early 1970s. Since no more than 200 Soviet cities then had a population so large the US possessed a significant "overkill" capacity.[40] The excess remained targeted as before on Russian military sites (i.e. counter-force targets). The US was, thus, saddled with a new and destabilising technology and the Soviet Union had an incentive to develop the MIRV technology as well, which it did some five years later.

The development of MIRV induced US strategic planners to re-think their deterrent strategy. In January 1974, Secretary of Defence James Schlesinger announced the policy of Flexible Targeting whereby America would modify its nuclear deterrent strategy to strikes only against military targets in response to a limited firing of Soviet missiles against US military targets.[41] This fresh nuclear doctrine was promulgated by the National

---

38. John L Gaddis, *Strategies of Containment : A Critical Appraisal of Post-War American National Security Policy* (New York : Oxford University Press, 1982), p.279.
39. Ibid, p.280.
40. Ibid.
41. A new contingency plan for nuclear war was drawn up in SIOP-5. Read Peter Pringle, et al., *SIOP : The Secret US Plan for Nuclear War* (New York : W.W. Norton, 1984), p. 179.

Security Decision Memorandum 242 (NSDM). This doctrine provided for a more credible deterrent and escalation control through the development of a wider array of planned limited nuclear options. A principal component of this doctrine was the emphasis on destruction of Soviet economic recovery capabilities. However, the ability to destroy urban industrial targets continued to be indisposable. As Schlesinger himself put it in 1975 : "Even after a more brilliantly executed and devastating attack than we believed our potential adversary could deliver, the US could retain the capacity to destroy more than 75% of Soviet industries."[42] The cardinal idea behind the new policy, as explained, was that in a moment of national crisis, the President needed a 'menu' of options rather than launching an all-out attack against the Soviet Union or taking no action at all.

Schlesinger's arguments that nuclear war could be kept limited were challenged by many. As to why the Soviets would take the terrible risk of launching a limited nuclear attack in the first place, he had no explanation. Further, Kremlin could hardly be sure of an equally limited retaliation. Even if American retaliation were limited it could still be severe and hostilities would not be likely to end there.[43] Kissinger wrote in 1965: "No one knows how the government or people will react to a nuclear explosion under conditions where both sides possess nuclear arsenals."[44]

It was not clear whether this strategy of selective options meant the capability to strike Soviet military targets in general

---

42. Scott Sagan, *Moving Targets : Nuclear Strategy and National Security* (Princeton, N J: Princeton University Press, 1989), p.46.
43. R C Alridge, *First Strike : The Pentagon's Strategy for Nuclear War* (Boston : South End Press, 1983), pp. 33-34.
44. H Kissinger, *Problems of National Security* (New York : Praeger, 1965), p.6.

or the land-based missile silos in particular. Schlesinger's policy was given the official name "Flexible Targeting". Critics called it "a little nuclear war searching for a place to happen". In the sense of the latter statement, it would, as Smoke says, represent "a great change in American strategy".[45]

Carter and PD-59

A Nuclear Targeting Policy Review (NTPR) was conducted, which resulted in American strategy of nuclear deterrence being further elaborated during the Carter administration through Presidential Directive-59, issued in July 1980.[46] It was the foremost executive order requiring the US armed forces to fight an attenuated nuclear war and to illustrate America's ability to respond in a credible fashion without having to escalate instantaneously to an all-out nuclear war. The US would fine-tune its nuclear responses, especially against the military targets, with the intention of escalating gradually and to hold larger portions of nuclear warheads in reserve. It assigned priority to hardened underground shelters that would be used by the leaders in the event of a nuclear war. The US had begun to emphasise "nuclear decapitation".

This was a shoot-look-shoot capability. The main idea was for limited strikes against political and economic targets rather than exclusively against military targets. This policy officially christened 'Countervailing Strategy', remained the main arm of the American nuclear strategy under the Carter and Reagan administrations. The biggest difference that PD-59 introduced, Secretary of Defence Harold Brown explained to Congress in September 1980, is a specific recognition that "strategy has to

45. Richard Smoke, *National Security and the Nuclear Dilemma: An Introduction to the American Experience* (Massachusetts: Addison Wesley Publishing Co., 1984).
46. Roger Speed, *Strategic Deterrence in the 1980s* (Stanford: Hoover Institution Press, 1979).

be aimed at what Soviets think is important to them" and not just what the US would think is important to them (US) in the Soviet view.[47] This policy drew flak for four reasons. First, the capability to destroy hard targets cannot be differentiated from that needed to launch an all-out attack on Soviet Union. Second, the Soviets could easily have followed the American lead. Third, if the Soviets feared annihilation in the midst of a crisis, logic would dictate a pre-emptive strike. Fourth, it would create a threat to strike on command and control, communications and intelligence, which only ensures that the command centres of both powers would contribute to East-West tensions and make nuclear war more likely, by accident or miscalculation.[48]

The Reagan Administration

A new SIOP, designated SIOP-6, came into effect on October 1, 1983, integrating as in other SIOPs, new targets. It included some 50,000 potential target installations compared to about 25,000 in 1974 as contained in SIOP-5. The new SIOP divided targets into four categories, each of which contained a wide range of target types. The four principle groups were – Soviet nuclear forces, general purpose forces, Soviet military-political leadership centres, and Soviet economic and industrial base.[49]

The SIOP-6F came into force in October 1989. It brought in the most extensive revision of American nuclear war plans in a decade. It emphasised the destruction of Soviet leadership, described to consist of "some 100000" people. Considering the fact that the coming of Gorbachev in 1985 saw the initiation of 'Glassnost' and 'Perestroika' and the eventual culmination of the dissolution of the Warsaw Pact

47. Sagan, n.42, p.49.
48. Robert Scheer, *With Enough Shoves: Reagan, Bush and Nuclear War* (New York: Random House, 1982)
49. The most comprehensive writing on nuclear targeting in my opinion is Desmond Ball's *Strategic Nuclear Targeting,* p.80

and the demise of the Soviet Union, this new SIOP was still suited to the 'evil' days of the Cold War. What they projected was what seemed to be an insensitivity to the changes in global, political and strategic environment.[50]

"The strategy of limited counter-force", writes Allen Krass, "is built entirely on hope;...hope that control can be maintained; hope that once a war starts both sides will be able to recognize a common point at which all cost-benefit calculations balance and they can stop it; but, above all, hope that 'when the time comes', when it is 'eye ball-to eye ball', they will blink first and we 'win without a shot being fired'. These hopes have extremely fragile foundations".[51]

Technological development strikes at the root of stability posture. The growth of highly accurate delivery systems and warheads destabilise the deterrence posture by increasing fears of pre-emptive strikes leading to increasing readiness to use forces prior to facing destruction at the hands of the adversary. The availability of accurate weapon systems increase pressures for counter-force targeting, which in turn require more warheads and delivery systems. It was through technological development that the number of targets in American warplans increased from 70 in 1949 to 50,000 or more by the 1980s.[52]

There was an endeavour "to increase the element of threat to the maximum while decreassing the risk to use to the minimum." This self-contradictory effort was like "trying to make use of the shadow of an object without having the object itself." It was against this background of confusion

50. Desmond Ball and Robert C Toth, " Revising the SIOP", *International Security* (Spring 1990), Vol.14, No.4, pp.65-92, at p.73.
51. Allan Krass, "The Evolution of Military Technology and Deterrence Strategy", *SIPRI* (London, 1981), p.40.
52. Malcolm Dando and Paul Rogers, *The Death of Deterrence* (London: CND Publication, 1984).

and discord that the peace movements of the early 1980s arose. For members of the peace movement, nuclear deterrence began to look "like a death sentence for the human race."[53] The contradiction within deterrence led to serious challenges to its postulates and underlying assumptions, especially in early 1980s. "The inescapable truth", observed Schell, "was that possession inevitably implied use and use was ...senseless."[54]

By the 1980s, some pillars of the American national security establishment themselves began to challenge the basic postulates of American nuclear deterrence strategy. George Kennan made a passionate appeal to those engaged in the game. "For the love of God, of your children, and of civilization to which you belong", he appealed, "cease this madness, you have a duty not just to the generation of the present. You have a duty to civilizations past, which you threaten to render non-existent. You are mortal men. You are capable of error. You have no right to hold in your hands...destructive powers sufficient to put an end to civilized life on a great portion of your planet. No one should wish to hold such powers".[55]

A group of former NATO Generals and Admirals first met in 1981 and formed the group called Generals for Peace and Disarmament. They had begun challenging nuclear deterrence. Admiral Sanguinetti stated thus:-

"A man who has witnessed a nuclear explosion asks no further questions but changes his thinking habits radically. He realizes once and for all that he is no longer dealing with explosives, not even in massive or gigantic dosages. One is

53. Jonathan Schell, *The Abolition* (New York: Knopf, 1984), p.67.
54. Ibid, p.66.
55. George F Kennan, *The Nuclear Delusion: Soviet and American Relations in the Atomic Age* (London: Hamish Hamilton, 1984), p.144.

overawed in the face of a horrible and inconceivable catastrophe that has been triggered by man but cannot be controlled by him. It does not matter which side you are on, you will never use the same arguments you did before. I personally witnessed six nuclear explosions".

The French President, Giscard d'Estaing, hurriedly discharged Generals Bollardiere, Binoche and Admiral Sanguinetti, when they openly criticised French and NATO nuclear policies. But the danger of an atomic war set limits to military obedience. The soldier may have to face the dilemma of what to obey first – the fundamental human right to live in peace or the order to use nuclear weapons as a last resort.[56]

A major figure in the peace movement described deterrence as a "pitiful, lightweight theory...espoused in its pristine purity, only by a handful of monkish celibates, retired within the walls of centers of strategic studies. It cannot endure any intercourse with the actual world. It appears always as a gloss, as a theoretical legitimisation of actions, which are taken for quite different reasons."[57] He maintained that its major procedures were predictive, yet its predictions were of a kind which could never be verified or falsified. It was not a branch of scholarship but scholasticism, whose practitioners were trapped within the enclosed circularity of their own self-validating logic.[58]

---

56. Generals for Peace and Disarmament, *A Challenge to US/NATO Strategy* (New York: University Books, 1984). Introduction by Michael N Harbottle, Foreword by Admiral Gene R LaRouque, USN (Retd), p.22.
57. E P Thompson, "Deterrence and Addiction", in Thompson, *Beyond the Cold War* (New York: Pantheon, 1982), pp.1-23.
58. Ibid.

The Strategic Defence Initiative

On March 23, 1983, President Reagan gave a speech on the "vision of the future which offers hope." "Would it not be better", he argued, "to save lives than to avenge them? Are we not capable of demonstrating our peaceful intentions by applying all our abilities and our ingenuity to achieving a truly lasting stability. I think we are ... indeed we must."[59]

This idea "revolutionized the strategic debate in the US without changing the world's nuclear arsenals in the slightest."[60] With this speech, Reagan in fact stole the moral high ground from the peace movement and the Pastoral Letter of the American Catholic Bishops. He did so in a manner that appealed to the American isolationist and technological optimism.[61]

The casual chatter of the members of the first Reagan administration about nuclear warning shots and 'prevailing' in a nuclear war had produced an undercurrent of general public unease, which resulted in the sudden popularity of the movement in the United States to freeze the existing nuclear stockpiles, leading to the eventual reduction and possibility of elimination of thermonuclear armouries. It also generated a massive peace movement in Western Europe.

An additional complication for the nuclear warriors was the difficulty in finding a suitable basing mode for the MX missiles. At the beginning of the 1980s, the missile was alone estimated to cost about $10 bn. Construction of 4,600 shelters for it was to add another $16 bn. The 200 missile sites would have required the construction of 8000 miles of roadways in addition to the shelters and command facilities. The gigantic enterprise called for 600,000 tonnes of cement, between 32

---

59. *New York Times,* March 24, 1983.
60. Scott Sagan, *Moving Targets: Nuclear Strategy and National Security* (Princeton, NJ.: Princeton University Press, 1989), p.46.
61. E P Thompson, *Star Wars* (Harmondsworth: Penguin Books, 1985), p.99.

to 48 million tonnes of sand, 210 million gallons of liquid asphalt, 125 million gallons of fuel and 17.9 bn gallons of water. The Mormon Church expressed its vehement opposition to the construction of the missile. Lieutenant General Daniel O Graham, former Director of the Defence Intelligence Agency and founder of a lobby for space-based defence called the High Frontier; Edward Teller, a veteran of the Manhattan Project during the Second World War, which resulted in the atomic bomb and the so-called Father of the H-bomb; Admiral James Watkins, Chief of Naval Operations; Reagan's so-called Kitchen Cabinet, which consisted of Karl Bendetsen – a retired businessman and a former Assistant Secretary of the Army; William Wilson – a rancher and an oil-man; and Joseph Coors – a beer magnate; this privileged group of elderly advisors influenced Reagan more than his regular advisors within the administration. George Keyworth, his science advisor and a protégé of Edward Teller, was "surprised, shocked and even stunned" when he was told on March 19, 1983, that the President wanted to know whether "it was a good time to renew efforts in strategic defense". Despite his early misgivings and advice by his scientific colleagues that he should "fall on the sword" and resign, Keyworth prudently supported the President's search for strategic defence.[62]

Reagan had announced a major revolution in the nuclear orders based on the supremacy of the offensive without an analytical effort within his scientific and strategic bureaucracies

---

62. There could hardly be a more comprehensive and neat account than provided for by my JNU Professor, Professor M Zuberi, in his excellent but underrated article "Swords and Shields : A Scientific Controversy", *Man and Development* (March 1991). Most of this portion is as was in the article, because it is near impossible to improvise on what has been written by him. It is nearly never possible to do so anyway.

and without any consultations with the governments of America's military allies.

An underlying idea was to devise a defensive technology that would restore the protective insularity of the United States threatened by essential equivalence in offensive thermonuclear armouries between the United States and the Soviet Union. 'Star Wars' promised to regain the moral high ground which the critics of nuclear strategy had claimed for themselves. "Star Wars", said E P Thompson, "is the ultimate decomposition of the deterrence theory, and the attempt by the United States nuclear ideologists to return to the womb of Hiroshima."[63] Edward Teller had in the past advocated work on the hydrogen bomb, an offensive weapon, and now he supported research on defensive weapons. The hydrogen bomb was a single weapon being pushed by its supporters within the closed circle of decision makers. Strategic defence was to be based on the co-ordinated operation of a whole series of weapon systems and devices. The most obvious similarity between the decisions is a resort to technological fix for a security problem, which is primarily political. The main difference is that while a strategy had to be devised to accommodate the awesome power of the H-bomb, the SDI demanded technological innovation to satisfy the requirements of strategy. The scientists engaged in research for SDI were driven by intellectual curiosity and technological challenge "reaching into exotic regimes of high energy physics, where they deal with cataclysmic energies, distant frontiers of computer science and remotest reaches of sensing and communications." Having recognised that there is little more to be done in improving offensive weapons, Hans Bethe remarked, "they are enthusiastic advocates of defensive weapons and in this advocacy they

63. Ibid, p.46.

are finding a very receptive government." "We are working on weapons of life", said Larry West, "ones that will save people from the weapons of death."[64]

Keeny and Panofsky argue that for such a system to work effectively, it must be "leakproof", since the penetration of even a single warhead would cause tremendous destruction. They observe thus:

"...a single modern strategic weapon could have a million times the yield of the high explosive strategic bombs of World War II, or one hundred to thousand times the yield of the atom bombs that destroyed Hiroshima and Nagasaki, killing 250,000 people."

Teller had argued, as early as in 1963, in favour of such high altitude nuclear testing in order to devise an X-ray laser pumped into outer space by nuclear explosions to destroy missiles in flight. Teller maintained that a leak-proof defence against missiles is not possible. What the United States must aim at, according to him, is "some defense, not a perfect defense." Reagan's idea of an "impenetrable umbrella" was based on the development of such new technologies as laser and particle beam weapons. However, the particle beam weapons were still in the conceptual stage.[65]

The intensity of the scientific opposition can be seen by the fact that when alternative sources of research support were dwindling, thousands of scientists had pledged not to accept any funding from the Star Wars project. By the Spring of 1986, 3,700 professors and 2,800 junior faculty members had signed the pledge. In November 1985, it was revealed

---

64. S M Keeny and W K H Panofsky, "MAD versus NUTS", *Foreign Affairs* (Winter 1981-82), p.291.
65. Kosta Tsipis, *Arsenal: Understanding Weapons in the Nuclear Age* (New York: Simon & Schuster, 1983), p. 211.

that there were some unresolved difficulties regarding measuring some properties of X-ray laser.[66] There were also some problems regarding the complex requirements of battle management systems. It was estimated that 25 to 61 million lines of error-free computer code would be needed for the system, ie the size of 100 text books. There were some programming errors too, compounded by the fact that the software would be based on assumptions about the adversary's capabilities and plans. Even a single computer miscalculation could lead to a computer-generated holocaust. "A weapon you can't trust", stated David Parnas, "is of no use to you. We will make decisions as if it were not there, and they will make decisions as if it might work."[67]

Robert McNamara, who as the Defence Secretary had contributed considerably to American defence policy and during whose tenure one witnessed a steady build up of American weapon systems, observed that "nuclear weapons have no military purpose whatsoever ... except only to deter one's opponent from using them."[68]

66. Zuberi, n.62, p.68.

67. Ibid, p. 50.

68. Robert Strange McNamara, "The Military Role of Nuclear Weapons: Perceptions and Misperceptions", *Foreign Affairs* (Fall 1983), p. 79.

3

The Doctrine of Just War

It is nearly four decades since John XXIII issued the *Pacem in Terris* and as many years since the Vatican II called for an "entirely new attitude" towards war. This attitude reflects the pacifism and non-violence that characterised the thinking of early Christians. Pacifism is essentially a complex of perceptions leading to or derived from Christian faith. These perceptions are the perception of God ; the perceived relationship between devotees and God; and the objective of that relationship.

For the pacifist, wars do come as a result of human error but his God never chooses this option of devastation to show displeasure. Success and failure, for a pacifist, lie with God.[1] The theory and practice of non-violence has, thus, been the key to the pacifist alternative to war. The pacifist's insistence upon non-violent resistance is a refusal to succumb to the delusion of succeeding over evil by adding to it. This sense of confidence in "abandonment' is grounded in the belief that God's power will be made perfect in our eternity – however hopeless a situation appears, God's vengeance will not be omnipresent. For the pacifist, this offers greater security

1. Gordon C Zahn, "Pacifism and Just War" in Philip J Murnion (ed), *Catholics and Nuclear War : A Commentary on the Challenge of Peace : The US Catholic Bishops Pastoral Letter* (New York : Crossroad, 1983).

than reliance on nuclear deterrence. But the very fact that 'much is left to be decided by the Almighty' makes pacifism seem lost in some sort of hopelessness. It would, however, be wrong to assume pacifism to be unrealistic or to think that nuclear pacifists are devoid of awareness of policy issues.[2]

Pacifists hold the primacy of religious commitment over national identities and loyalties. According to them, Christians must refrain from participating in violent exchanges and work for removing disparities in society, thus removing the root cause of conflict. Pacifists agree on the importance of diplomacy and peaceful solutions but they are likely to put more emphasis on self-confession and mutual understanding. Pacifism also calls for an expanded definition of the concept of common good. For the pacifists, the state too is bound by the limits of morality and is not above the citizen.

Pacifists are vociferous objectors to the production, possession and use of nuclear weapons. These forbidden acts are a "crime second only to the Crucification of Christ.[3] The state, whose prime function is to meet the needs of the individuals, could hardly take up functions destructive of the common good. For the pacifist, even the risk of national defeat, loss of freedom, sacrifices, hardships are better than a prospect of a final holocaust. Reaching out to the potential enemy and self-analysis could lead to a response in kind. For him, politics has made diplomacy a continuation of war by other means, contrary to Clausewitz's view of war as an instrument of diplomacy.

The theory of pacifism was an obvious though unconscious device by which behaviour of Christians could be

---

2. Gordon Zahn, "Violence and Pacifism" in *War Conscience and Dissent* (London: Geoffrey Chapman, 1967), p. 100.
3. Thomas Merton, *The Non-Violent Alternative* (New York : Farrar, Strauss and Giroux, 1980), p. 75.

accommodated to the needs of the state. Ironically, there is no answer for Christians killing Christians.

Nuclear Pacifism

The nuclear pacifist sanctions the use of violence as a 'last resort'. However, there is disagreement amongst themselves on the issue of deciding which dispute warrants the use of violence, and how much. They agree that the non-use of nuclear weapons is legitimate. For them, nuclear weapons serve no military or defensive purpose. This is their conclusion reached on the basis of cost, proportionality and discrimination. They are critical of the doctrine of nuclear deterrence and the problems associated with it. They prefer to pursue alternatives to nuclear weapons. After all, their objective is the stabilisation of relations and maintenance of peace amongst conflicting nations. According to them, easier options are possible in lieu of relying solely on the means of defence that would destroy societies politically, economically, socially, psychologically and ecologically.

The central problem is that of an adequate philosophical orientation towards the nature of war itself. War is not a generalised violence; there are certain self-imposed and other limitations attached to it though they hardly weaken it.[4] This intrinsic imperative towards control is derived from the need to maintain order and discipline in order to conserve moral and material forces.[5] The difficulty, however, lies in maintaining restraints derived from criteria other than those inherent in sound strategy and the requirement for good order and military discipline. The first criteria dominated the politics of

4. Karl Von Clausewitz, *On War* trans. Peter Paret & Michael Howard (Princeton : Princeton University Press, 1977), p.75.
5. Michael Howard, "Temperamenta Belli : Can War be Controlled?" in his book, *Restraints on War : Studies in the Limitations of Armed Conflict* (Oxford : Oxford University Press, 1979), pp. 3-4.

ecclesiastical influence in Europe till the 16th century when the necessities of warfare were accommodated to the moral code of conduct set up for Christians. The second criteria was from the 17th to 19th century – the age of Grotious, when it was assumed that law of nations was founded on the perception that in peacetime, nations ought to do maximum good, and in time of war, minimum injury without minimising their own real interests.

The Just War Doctrine

Just War theory was formed out of the Medieval Just War doctrine, which itself was a product of distinct religious and secular traditions:-

- Post-Reformation 'Holy War' doctrine — where just war is coded as a 'Crusade'.[6]
- Concepts formulated in the 16th and 17th centuries and developed into secular international laws.

The Just War doctrine is a "mosaic of thought fashioned by theologians, philosophers, jurists, statesmen and soldiers."[7] This doctrine is the result of several centuries of struggle. The theoretical and the practical have intermingled at every stage in the historical development of this tradition.[8] The origins of Just War doctrine are normally traced from the early history of the Christian Church and its acceptance of the need to defend the spiritual realm within the temporal.[9] Augustine of Hippo laid down certain conditions and

6. Roland Bainton, *Christian Attitudes Towards War and Peace* (Nashville, Tennesse : Abingdon Press, 1960).
7. D L Davidson, *Nuclear Weapons and the American Churches* (Boulder, Colorado : Westview Press, 1983), p.13.
8. James Turner Johnson, *Can Modern War be Just?* (New Haven, Conn: Yale University Press, 1977), p.17.
9. Ian Clarke, *Waging War : A Philosophical Introduction* (Oxford, UK: Clarendon Press, 1988), p. 32.

circumstances under which war could be justified with limitations on the harm that could be done even in wars that were justified. This is regarded as the conception of the Just War doctrine in Christian teaching and the foundation for Western thought regarding restraint on war. The doctrine consists of traditional scholastic Just War theory enriched by the contemporary social teaching of the Catholic Church on war, the teaching of the Protestants, the moralists, the philosophers, to which one must add the positive international law of war which has been developing since the 17th century. What we encounter in Just War tradition is a multifaceted conglomeration of moral insights and practices regarding the experience and judgements of historical persons, across the borders and the whole breadth of cultural institutions.[10]

In regard to Just War it is neigh impossible to forego the writings of James Turner Johnson. He has maintained that the Just War doctrine in its classical from does not exist in either Augustine, theologians or Canonists of the high middle ages. It can be traced from the end of middle ages (by roughly 1500 AD).[11] The term *bellum justum* is derived from Roman Law and is an interesting blend of the religious and legal ideas, representing a war decided and executed in adherence to the necessary formalities. But in the Roman 'Just War', legal form was an adjunct of religious practice. It was expected that God would assist in the conduct of war.[12]

Aristotle regards waging of war as a prerequisite to maintaining peace. He advanced the intellectual and moral

---

10. Johnson, n.8.
11. Special reference to J T Johnson's book, *Ideology, Restraint and Limitations of War* (Princeton : Princeton University Press, 1975), Chapter I.
12. F H Russell, *The Just War in the Middle Ages* (Cambridge : Cambridge University Press, 1975), p.6.

virtues of restraint while exercising coercion.[13] Cicero, the Roman philosopher, elaborated and refined some of the standards of moral réstraint which were based on natural law.[14] "We are born for Justice based upon Nature." Since Roman times there has been a productive inter-relationship between *jus naturale* (Natural Law), and *jus gentium* ie the law of the people, of nations. The fundamental concern of Just War tradition was not regarding what men did in war but what they ought to refrain from doing, based on natural law reasoning.[15] In fact, the Christians attempted to combine biblical teachings with Graeco-Roman Just War notions vis-à-vis the realities of international politics. The utterance of the Old Testament in the Bible, that wars are initiated under the guidance of God,[16] is in total contrast to Paul's defence of the right of states to use the sword.[17] As a result, Christians had to co-ordinate three positions on use of armed forces:-

- Emphasis of Jesus on peace and non-violent methods.
- Holy-war doctrine of Old Testament.
- Just War doctrine of classical Graeco-Roman tradition.

Medieval Period

The Medieval Just War doctrine, rather than being ecclesiastical in origin was a confluence of the religious, chivalric and secular ideas fashioning Just War components into an integral whole. While the religious notion conceded the right to wage war, the content of the secular doctrines related to the proper mode of fighting.[18] It is this modified doctrine of the Medieval

---

13. Aristotle, *Nicomachean Ethics* (New York : Bobs-Merill Inc, 1962), p.90.
14. Cicero, *Laws*, Trans, Clinton Walker - Keya (Cambridge, Mass : Harvard University Press, 1927), pp.1 & X.
15. William V. O'Brien, *The Conduct of Just and Limited War* (New York: Praeger 1981), pp. 4 -5.
16. *Old Testament* (Deutronomy), Chapter 7 ; Verse 16.
17. Paul's Letter, *New Testament* (Romans), Chapter 8.
18. Johnson, n.11, p.9.

Ages that is the classic Just War tradition that conditioned the thinking of the 16th and 17th century theorists.[19] The gradual amalgamation of these traditions in the late Medieval Ages has a counterpart in the dissolution of classic Just War doctrine in the century following Reformation. At the root of this classic Just War doctrine lies the fundamental postulate that there must be a grave fault on one side and vindicative justice on the other to be undertaken by the "minister of God", who could even be a prince. This became the central character (though not the central concept) of the doctrine in the Medieval Ages, along with the statement that justice expressed itself not just through vindication but through mercy too. It also set limits on what "God's ministers" may do. Medieval Christianity produced an *ad bellum* but the *jus in bello* came out of the sensibilities of the knightly class.

It was St Augustine who went on to structure the framework for medieval reflections and reinterpreted the New Testament of the Bible. Christians could take up arms as an exercise in "benevolent severity" – if done in the right spirit. War and conquest came to be regarded as sad necessities in the eyes of men of principle. A Just War was nothing but an action to restore a violated moral order.[20]

St Augustine agreed with Aristotle, Cicero and other classical authors that the exercise of government entailed the administration of regulation of force – just use of force was possible only if the following questions were asked and satisfactory answers could be obtained:-

- Who decreed the recourse to force?
- What reasons prompted such order?

19. Ibid., p.46.
20. R S Hartigan, "St Augustine on War and Killing", *Journal of the History of Ideas* (April / June 1996), p.199 quoted in Clarke, n.9, p.33.

- What were the other conditions that governed decision to use force?
- What was the acceptable conduct of armed conflict with regard to armed and unarmed people?

To St Augustine, the rightful authority to declare use of force would be the ruler or authorised civil magistrate. But it must be in assertion of the gravest consequence, for later Just War teaching held that the Church could use coercion indirectly to protect and promote the religion. "Reasons for the use of force could vary from averting injuries against aggressive attacks, against wrongful seizure of assets, against past wrongs. Each of these purposes would differ regarding the degree of permissiveness in war's conduct. However, this crucial innovation was to specify offences against the Christian teaching as a valid reason for employing force (persecution of heretics, guilty of sacrilegious acts)."[21]

St Augustine gave great weightage to correct intentions on the part of those undertaking and participating in a conflict with the sole aim of achieving peace with justice. Without the character of restraint *jus in bello* could not have developed. Right intention was considered as sufficient justification provided the intention was to restore just peace. The concept of right intention, as Johnson states, can properly be conceived as an important source for the *jus in bello* in Christian theological thought. St Augustine, however, had the tendency to make its prosecution limitless.

St Augustine moderated the brutalities of warfare and gave the first hint of principle of "non-combatant immunity" though he neither developed not elaborated it. This moral distinction later took on the greatest significance in the Just War tradition. However, any violation of Christian doctrine

21. This provided the foundation for the just use of force against Muslims and other heretics and 'infidels', after the 11th century.

merited punishment of even those who were morally innocent. This distinction is inherent in the classical and in the Stoic tradition of natural justice, which referred to certain incontestable ways of treating people. Since the conduct of war was bound by limitations of weapons technology in the Medieval period, there was no felt need to proceed to elaborate a separate set of principles for its conduct.

"The fusion of religious, chivalric and secular ideas gave spiritual sanction to military enterprise and knightly protection to the Church. It also reinforced the authority of the prince as the only legitimate source of military command." It is for this reason that certain critics maintain that Just War doctrine was nothing but a conglomeration of principles of self-interest to serve a particular society and to maintain a particular status quo.

During St Augustine's time, the Christian Church came to embody the conflict. On one hand, the Church was the depository of non-coercive belief and action. On the other hand, it could regulate or propagate its message by forceful means. This contradiction inherent in St Augustine's writings remained throughout the Medieval Ages. The pacifist's tradition was not predominant during this period. The lesson to be learnt, Francis Bacon, an English Fransiscan, argued was that war against unbelievers would anger them more against the Christian faith rather than convert them.

The 13th century opened the way for serious consideration of the problems of consolidating and clarifying the position of the Church on war. This position was based on *Corpus Juris* (code of cannon law) which included *Decretals* of Gratian and the *Summa Theologica* of Thomas Acquinas. From these compilations flow two streams of thought which shaped the Just War doctrine during rest of the Medieval Ages — Scholastic Theology and Canon Law. The latter is also inherent in secular law — an important factor in late 14th and 15th centuries.

The Holy War Crusaders

The middle ages witnessed two limitations within the confines of which the doctrine of Just War developed. These were the Christian doctrine as shaped in the West, and the religious unification of Europe. The ideological nature (in a relativistic sense) of the doctrine of Just War worked successfully towards limiting conflicts within society. The peculiarly ideological notion of Just War is a notion of justice conditioned by theology, philosophical orientation and common custom. This period witnessed the theological and philosophical unity that characterised the West. After the Reformation and the emergence of two groups of Catholics and Protestants, just cause took the form of holy cause for the holy warriors.[22] It became a religious weapon against non-Christians.[23] For the Crusaders the threat to Christianity posed by unbelief was a justification for resort to force. This period witnessed the formalisation of *jus ad bellum* principle as between two states.

A relationship of reciprocity was applied to Europe and the Just War doctrine was utilised to specify when a just cause for war existed. This was also the period of colonialism and, for the first time, people of other regions came in contact with ideologies of what was once the monopoly of the West.

St Thomas Acquinas

St Thomas Acquinas was one of the earliest thinkers to emphasise the imperatives of restraint which were present in St Augustine's writings but disregarded by the Crusaders. It is in fact this factor that advanced Just War thinking. The religious

---

22. William Grange, *Gods' Three Arrows, 111 : The Churchs' Conquest over the Sword* (London : George Miller for Edward Brewster, 1631), p.231 in Johnson, n.8, p.16.
23. Russell, n.12, p.194

weapon for Acquinas was spiritual in nature and not a weapon of destruction.[24] The Church could not order the use of force, though it could induce others to wage a war. The spiritual domain was superior to the natural order, yet the natural order, which encompassed the political and the legal had autonomous authority. The Prince had independent authority to run his affairs even if he were an infidel or an 'unbeliever'. Right authority existed where the Magistrate was acting as the minister of God. Acquinas does not question what is right in war. For him, Just War should be defensive in nature. He also justifies use of force in certain non-military disputes.

Acquinas qualified the religious causes and reinforced the importance of secular and temporal causes of war. According to him, a just cause for war existed when there was a fault that required punishment; "where the poor and the commonwealth had to be defended from the injustice to be inflicted by the enemy."[25] The concept of right intention, drawn from the views of St Augustine, requires the Christians to love their enemies, not hurt or dominate them. This could be rightly considered as an important source for *jus in bello*.

All these preconditions pertained to *jus ad bellum* – whether a Just War could be begun, and whether a Christian could take up arms in the first place (not on what they may do after the war had begun). Till the 16th century this was the principal content of the Just War doctrine. On the question of whether unbelief constituted an intolerable offence, highlighted by the Crusaders, St Acquinas considered belief to be a matter between the person and his conscience. To conquer this unbelief was senseless. Unwilling belief, he maintained, was impossible.[26] This became an important focal point in the subsequent thinking on Just War.

---

24. C D Smith, *The Hundred Percent Challenge : Building a National Institute of Peace – A Platform for Planning and Progam* (Washington D.C.: Seven Locks Press, 1985).
25. Ibid, p.17.
26. Eric D'Arcy, *Conscience and Its Right to Freedom* (London : Sheed & Ward, 1979), pp. 153-154.

Though extensive attention was not paid to restraint on the conduct of war, the beginnings of the principle of non-combatant immunity are implicit in the writings of Aquinas.[27] Not only is direct intentional killing of innocent persons condemned but even their indirect and unintentional killing is prohibited.[28] These views were interwoven with and influenced by the secular principles of the 'chivalric code'. However, Acquinas permits the enslavement of enemy prisoners, seizing of enemy's property and ambush in a 'just' war based on these conditions. A strict adherence to agreements made with the enemy(ies) is also considered absolutely necessary.

The Post-Medieval Reaction

"The segmentation of medieval society into numerous, independent, nation-states and the collapse of the geographical and political domains of the Roman Catholic Church had the profoundest effect upon the Just War tradition". The Church had served as a supranational court of appeal and source of compromise in political disputes and conflicts, and, consequently, Just War standards were, up to a point, authoritative and effective. So long as the Church remained the dominant institution, holy war image continued to exert enormous influence in contradiction to the pacific dispositions of the early Church period and the restraining sentiments of classical Just War theory. By the 15th and 16th centuries, the demise of respected central authority left nations with standards regarding the use of force that were susceptible to extensive partiality and bias.[29]

27. LeRoy B Walter, "Five Classic Just War Theories: Thomas Acquinas, Vitoria, Suarez, Gentilli and Grotius", in CD Smith, n. 24, p.18.
28. Johnson, n.11, p.131.
29. Ibid.

What is more, the medieval establishment encouraged the Church, despite some reluctance, to consider force as a legitimate means for manipulating the conscience and for punishing and dispossessing the unorthodox. The potency of the holy war tradition did not expire with the collapse of medieval society. After the Reformation, it continued to fire the imaginations of some reformers and their followers. The Reformed tradition reveals a particularly 'acute ambivalence' over the use of force. However, John Calvin and many of his followers shared the medieval enthusiasm for an established, uniform Church. That very enthusiasm for bringing Church and sword into close alliance, when replicated among conflicting religious groups and territories, helped to generate the bloody and protracted wars of religion, as well as the wars of imperial expansion and colonisation so characteristic of the post-medieval period.

But given the diversity of contending attitudes towards war and peace within the tradition, the crusading spirit did not go unchallenged. The 16th and 17th centuries were a particularly creative period for the advocates of restraint. The modern Just War doctrine, which began in the 16th century, played down the themes of fault and vindictive justice and stressed the confines of what could be done in a just cause. Consequently, Just War doctrine was pulled in two directions, separating vindication and mercy, which had existed together in the Medieval Age. The influential writings of early modern Just War thinkers – both Catholic and Protestants – such as Francisco de Vitoria, Francisco Suarez, Alberico Gentilli, and Hugo Grotius are in many ways elaborate explanations on this statement.

For the theorists of the modern period, it was not the teaching of the Bishop of Hippo but the Just War doctrine, which had been shaped for many centuries especially by Canonists and theologians,[30] which influenced their thinking.

30. Johnson, n.8, p.34. Most of the text quoted or penned here is taken from the writings of James Turner Johnson.

They articulated something of St Augustine's earlier anguish over combat and were consumed with the cause of international peace. In the opinion of Grotius, men rush to take up arms for slightest of causes, or for no cause at all. Once force is resorted to, there is no respect for law[31] – be it divine or human.[32] Therefore, war must be undertaken only for the enforcement of rights, and once undertaken, it should be carried on within the confines of law and good faith.[33] These theorists of the modern period also reasserted and elevated natural law as the basic standard for the just administration of force. They restricted the use of religious causes in legitimating force, though with different degrees of stringency. The strong drive during this period to respect the 'natural' rights of conscience, possession, and self-government of people is, therefore, linked directly to the declining appeal of the holy war.

Grotius rejected medieval notions of collective guilt and punishment. He even suggests that if there exists a strong doubt about the justifiability of resort to force in some case, the citizen has the right to disobey; it is a lesser evil and a better option than manslaughter. Critical of secrecy in the initiation of hostilities, he emphasised that all attempts at justification of resort to arms 'ought to be clear and open.' In the interest of moderating what Grotius saw as the "frenzy" of violence that had seized post-medieval Europe, he and the others attempted to elaborate and refine the four general categories of Just War concerns that had been struggling for existence for a long time.

The Just War Principles

These principles of Just War doctrine are an amalgamation of formulations in different ways during different phases of

31. Hugo Grotius, *Problegomena to the Law of War and Peace*, trans. Francis W Kelsey (New York : Liberal Arts Press, 1957), p.21.
32. Grotius, *The Rights of War and Peace*, trans, F.W. Kelsey (Oxford : Clarendon Press, 1925), Ch.I, "What is Lawful in War".
33. Ibid.

the tradition. They primarily fall into two broad groups - the *jus ad bellum* refers to the justification of war, *jus in bello* refers to the limitation of war. *Jus ad bellum* explores whether the grounds for the initiation of armed hostilities are grave enough to warrant an overriding of the prima facie obligation of non-violence. *Jus in bello* governs the judgement regarding the use of particular means during a war.

Problems that arise in the *jus in bello* context cause us to reflect more about the nature of values, the threat against them, and the best methods to be used to protect and preserve them. To identify and solve these concerns we again look to the decision to go to war, ie the *ad bellum.*[34] Though *ad bellum* and *in bello* cannot be demarcated on strict lines, the logical and historical priority is with the former. It is only after the former is dealt with, that the question of latter arises.

In regard to legitimate authority there is a new and stronger emphasis upon the responsibility of secular rulers in matters of war and peace along with an undeniable reduction of the temporal role of the Church. By the term 'right authority' Augustine implies – the ends of good government.[35]

"The historic function of the requirement...was...to limit exactly the kind of unrestrained general violence and indiscriminate destruction that typically characterised civil wars". For the Canonists, it was the means to restrict resort to force and avoid the consequential destruction that accompanies it. Catholics like Suarez and Vitoria still ascribed some authority to the Pope in resolving international disputes

34. O'Brien has emphasised the difference between "war decision – *ad bellum*" and war fighting – *in bello,* in order of priority, in his book, *The Conduct of Just and Limited War,* n.15, Chapters 1-3.
35. Johnson, n.8, p.22.

and in recommending the use of force where the Church was threatened.[36] New conceptions of consent and popular sovereignty as the basis of political authority emerged. The fact that enforcement of justice was not a private prerogative of individuals but that of a legitimately constituted government was emphasised. This brought to the fore the complex relationship between moral precepts and political culture.[37]

In cases of revolutionary insurrection, where the government has forfeited its legitimacy due to persistent oversight of justice and violation of its citizen's human rights, this authority may be transferred to extra-governmental movements. Thinkers like Vitoria and Grotius had developed opinions that logically implied a justification, and in some cases, revolution. Gentilli and Grotius became less enthusiastic over the time about revolutionary stirrings. This problem of revolution was to remain a sore point for Just War thinking ever after. Vitoria forbade the state from making war for religion. On the other hand, colonisers used his emphasis on free passage for peaceful missionaries and traders, to their benefit. They had the right and the authority to use force if resisted in this "noble" cause. Grotius and Gentilli transformed the Just War doctrine's requirement of proper authority to wage war into a requirement that war be a public contest solemnly declared. By formalising the criterion of just cause, Grotius paved the way for acceptance of state sovereignty through the criterion of right authority. This identification of moral with the political made it more problematic to make sense of the moral notion of authority in the contemporary world.[38] Johnson rightly puts it – the requirement that there must be a right authority for use of force means that we must enquire whether there is any authority who can control the employment of force, so as to limit its

36. Ibid, p.23.
37. Johnson, n.11, p.61.
38. Ibid, p.23.

effects and behind that to enquire as to the breadth and depth of popular support this authority possesses.[39] As to the question of just cause, the use of force can only be for the protection of peace with justice, and not for vengeance or domination. Both in contemporary international law and in Roman Catholic thought since the times of Pope Pius XII, it has been further argued that the ferocity and destructiveness of war makes it necessary to limit the use of force as a means of defence against injustice. Aggressive wars, or initiated wars even in the cause of justice, are regarded as the most likely to unleash a total war making them incompatible with justice itself. Placing in the process, serious obstacles in the creation of international institutions that are imperative for genuine justice. The only just cause is in fact defence against unjust attacks.[40,41] Unfortunately, this itself is a subjective term that could be fashioned in the eye of the beholder.

Thus, the principle of just cause states that war is permissible to confront real and certain danger, to protect human life, to preserve the conditions for a decent existence and to secure basic human rights.[42] It can be traced in Christian thought as far back as St Augustine and has a history in the customs of pre-Medieval Germanic societies.

What can be observed is a strong emphasis upon "natural" or "moral" offence as a warrant for using force. There is only a vestigial reference to religious causes. The writers also make a distinction between 'self-defence' and a "defensive" war and punishment as an "offensive" one, broadened to include operations intended to "defend" foreign citizens against unjust rulers and defence of allies.[43]

---

39. Ibid, p.24.

40,41. A very interesting book on this aspect is that of John Courtney Murray, *Morality and Modern War* (New York : Council on Religious and International Affairs 1959), pp. 1-11, and, O'Brien, n.15, pp. 19-27.

42. Johnson, n.8, pp. 131-150.

43. Grotius, n.32, Book II, Chapter XX, p. 40.

There is no unanimity concerning the question of certifying or verifying the existence of a just cause. This was to become one of the most vexing problems for Just War theory, since belligerents are called upon, in effect, to try their own cases. Gentilli's view was that, so long as both sides "aim to justice", they may legitimately fight, despite any doubts. Grotius states that if there is any doubt at all about the causes of war, then force must be foresworn. This difference culminated in the equally controversial doctrine of 'simultaneously ostensible justice'. This was suggested by Vitoria according to which both sides in a war might well be justified. Vitoria spoke of 'invincible ignorance'. Belligerents are deceived into believing that each have a just cause, whereby neither may have a just reason (or else even the wrong side may believe they have a justified cause to fight). Vitoria believes that both sides may be treated as having a just cause and yet bound by *jus in bello*.[44] Grotius, for one, rejected the idea that from a moral point of view both sides could be equally right. But he did readily concede that one or both of the belligerents might understandably, if mistakenly, believe themselves to be in the right. He went on to counsel self-restraint and the need for both belligerents to declare their intents and claims publicly for all to sce and judge.[45]

The requirement of having a right intention is reduced somewhat in significance because of the preference of writers like St Augustine and Acquinas for evaluating deeds rather than motives.[46] It is an unqantifiable aspect and a subjective matter. However, since the only cause which can justify the resort to force is defence of justice, the intention of the belligerents must be limited to this end. Intention here concerns the purposes or ends which are sought to be served through

44. Johnson, n. 8, pp. 20-21.

45. Ibid, p.21.

46. A fairly rigorous analysis in David Fisher, *Morality and the Bomb* (London : Croom Helm, 1985), Chapter 6.

the use of force.[47] The only purpose which justifies the use of force is defence of justice and the promotion of genuine peace whose precondition is justice. Thus the requirement of right intention places limits on the purposes for which force may be employed.[48,49] It may not be used for purposes of dominance or vengeance, or in any way which makes just peace unattainable. The kind of intentionality that led Vattel and others to question the bombardment of cities with red hot cannon balls and other means was lost in the turbulent waters of total war represented by World War II.

The criterion of last resort is an evident corollary to the prima facie obligation not to injure human beings, until all reasonable means of solving a conflict peacefully have been exhausted. These include bilateral negotiations and full employment of regional and international mechanisms for conflict resolution. Johnson aptly puts it:

"The traditional idea that force must be the last resort thus carries with it the counsels of caution and prudence and serves as an implicit reminder that force may inspire more force, with the danger of loss of rational control over events. On the other hand (it) reminds us that the use of force may be a legitimate resort, when there are no other ways left to protect values that require to be preserved. Just war tradition thus points towards neither militarism nor pacifism, but to a state of affairs between these extremes."[50]

---

47. Alan Donagan, *The Theory of Morality* (Chicago : University of Chicago Press, 1977), pp. 122-127.

48,49. Obligation to non-violence continues to make a claim on our conscience, even when it is considered less stringent than the claims of justice. Refer O'Brien,n.15 pp. 33-35.

James Childress, "Just War Criteria", in Thomas A. Shannon, ed., *War or Peace ? : The Search for New Answers* (New York, Orbis : Maryknoll, 1980), pp. 48-49.

50. Johnson, n.11, p.24.

A resort to war must also conform to general proportionality. The values to be defended must be vital enough to outweigh the harm which accompany any use of force. On the other hand, the force employed must not do greater harm than the evil which is resisted. As William O'Brien points out :

"... There should be a balancing of effects on individual third parties and on the international common good. International interdependence means that international conflicts are difficult to constrain and that their shock waves affect third parties in a manner that must be accounted for in the calculus of probable good and evil..."[51]

A related test requires that there be a reasonable hope of success. This is a counsel of prudence. It would be irrational to undertake a costly and risky venture faced with the high probability of failure, given the presumption against violence shared by the theory of Just War and pacifism. This criterion not only calls for a reasonable assurance that justice will be achieved but also that the state of affected parties will not be worse off than before. There is a need for at least some reasonable confidence of a proportionate outcome. There is, of course, a greater or lesser element of uncertainty in any such estimate. This cannot be used to justify force on the ground of ignorance of the consequences. This criterion also includes a perception that at times maintaining key values even against odds may be a "proportionate" witness.[52]

Finally, there is a highly relevant criterion of the formal declaration of war, including a statement of charges. This, presumably, to assure full accountability. Given the speed with which the international events are unfolding, this criterion

---

51. O'Brien, n.15, p.27.
52. "The Challenge of Peace: God's Promise and Our Response: The Pastoral Letter of the American Catholic Bishops – 1983", para 94, in the *Strategic Digest* of November 1983.

could have run into problems already. The potential adversary requires every opportunity to change the course of events through serious political debates along with the consent of the defender country.

Legitimate authority, just cause, peaceful intention, last resort, general proportionality, reasonable hope of success, and formal declaration of war – these are the seven considerations that comprise a set of criteria that has come to be grouped under the appellation of *jus ad bellum.* These comprise the conditions that must be met before a decision to go to war is considered justified.

Certain additional conditions, present in the tradition but somewhat revised and systematised by the early modern theorists, make up a second category termed *jus in bello* – in other words, the permissible conduct of war. These dwell upon the ideas of proportionality and discrimination.

The *jus in bello* norms of the Just War theory set moral limits on the means that may be used even in a conflict that is itself justified under the *ad bellum criteria.* The fundamental principle behind the *jus in bello* criteria is the certitude that total or all out violence is never justified. "The single underlying requirement for the conduct of just war", states William O'Brien, "is that such a war must be limited."

Discrimination. The wisdom that underlies this criterion is that non-combatants must be immune from direct, intended, attack. Pacifism raises this conviction to the level of the absolute, while Just War theory, regretfully, agrees that some acts of killing are justified provided there is no threat to other human lives. But the intentional and direct killing of non-combatants is murder.[53]

53. For a careful scrutiny compare Paul Ramsey, *The Just War: Force and Political Responsibility* (New York: Charles Scribner's, 1968), Chapter 6 and O'Brien, n. 15, pp.42-55.

Although this criterion cannot be upheld absolutely, in any modern warfare, there is no justification for discarding it. Indiscriminate killing of non-combatants is a "crime against God and man himself".[54]

The limited war practice of the 18th century centred not on the immunity from harm but on restricting the area of military operations to avoid direct threats to the civilians of the warring nations. The early modern Just War thinkers permit the unintentional killing of innocent civilians and thereby introduce the so-called principle of 'double-effect'. It works as follows: If there are two effects of an action, one good and one bad, such as attacking a military installation, but in the process entailing unavoidable killing of several innocent civilians lodged therein, then the action is permissible, so long as the destruction of the installation is the only effect intended. The killing of the civilians is in that case regarded as a "collateral" side effect. The principle of side effect would rule out such terrorist acts as taking hostage or directly threatening lives of innocent civilians in order to exhort compliance from the enemy[55].

All these thinkers wrestled with the problem of defining "innocent civilians". They included the very young, the young, the old and the very old, the clerics, the monastics, farmers and so on – in fact "all those unable to bear arms". Moreover, they worried over "indiscriminate" weapons and they offered strictures against the use of wild animals and poison, because their effects were so hard to control. Discrimination was not

54. Ramsey argues for a non-combatant immunity as an absolute principle. O'Brien holds that it could in certain circumstances be subordinated to the demands of military necessity. He also favours the limitation of war which is doubtful in the light of his above interpretation of non-combatant immunity - unless both rivals are a rational and disciplined lot. The Pastoral Letter of the Vatican II in n.52, para 104.

55. See Smith, n. 24, pp. 24-25.

absolute for these writers. However, Johnson makes a poignant statement. "After any war", says he, "all persons are non-combatants, and the use of weapons that will forseeably endanger generations yet unborn...represents as much a violation of non-combatancy as a bullet through the brain of a child held hostage to cause an enemy to surrender."

Proportionality. The *in bello* criterion of proportionality demands that the harm caused by a particular military means must be outweighed by the values that it can reasonably be expected to protect.[56] However, this judgement of proportion does not balance the harm caused by a particular tactic against the good being defended by the war as a whole. Such an interpretation of the *in bello* proportionality would remove all restraint from the use of force in defence of a just cause. Michael Walzer observes that war is entirely and singularly the crime of those who begin it, and soldiers resisting aggression or rebellion can never be blamed for anything they do that brings victory closer. Correctly understood, proportionality as in *in bello* weighs the harm caused by the tactic in a Just War against the tactical advantages gained by this means.[57]

It, therefore, can only justify the use of military means for the pursuit of limited military objectives. If either of these limits is abandoned, war becomes total and unjust. For, in total war, the prima facie obligation of non-injury is not merely overridden in the defence of other values — it is denied outright and rendered irrelevant to moral decision-making. *Jus in bello* requires that any use of weapons should be, both, proportional and discriminate.

---

56. "The Challenge of Peace", n.52, para 105.
57. Ibid, pp.255-262. Also O'Brien, n.15, pp.39-40. Another interesting article to read on this aspect is by John C Ford, "The Morality of Obliteration Bombing", *Theological Studies*, 5 (1944), pp.261-309. He cites the case of Allied saturation bombing of Dresden in World War II that violated the *in bello* norms of discrimination and proportionality.

Force is at best a marginally defensible weapon for the pursuit of justice. Were justice a more important human value than non-violence, then the use of violence would be justified whenever the cause is 'just'. On the contrary, the Just War norms arise from a consideration of how the basic values of life, freedom, justice, etc are related to each other. They are a synthesis of, both, the political judgement and the moral commitment. The Just War criteria embody a representative tradition of Christian and humanist practical wisdom. One could not less agree with the verdict that all "ethical judgements in politics are historical judgements."[58]

58. Stanley Hoffman, *Duties Beyond Borders: On the Limits and Possibilities of Ethical International Politics* (Syracuse: Syracuse University Press, 1981), p.27.

4

Nuclear Deterrence and the Doctrine of Just War

I

We are discussing a doctrine whose primary intention is to prevent war and the secondary action is to ready those very actions that breach the principles of proportionality and discrimination and whose justification on the basis of this criteria, especially the former, must be subject to the most stringent analysis.[1] Nuclear deterrence rests on a compromise between logical opposites. It has confederated the prevention of war with the capability to fight, in the process conferring dignity on thermonuclear weapons and making people feel innocent. This led to moral euphoria and made the task of those who wanted to rid of these weapons more difficult.[2]

The fundamental issues have to do not only with nuclear war or accidents, but how these weapons are developed and deployed in the furtherance of the practice of nuclear

---

1. D B Fisher, *Morality and the Bomb* (London & Sydney: Croom Helm, 1985), p.72 ff.
2. M Zuberi, "Scientists, Social Scientists and the State of Nuclear Threat"; *Man & Development* (September 1986), pp.28-34, at p. 33.

deterrence. This discussion is with reference to the partially veiled tradition of Just War – that war and means of war must be justified and restrained by a concern to protect and preserve the values of utmost importance.

The doctrine of Just War refers to the rightness of going to war and the means to be used to fight in a war under certain conditions. A 'just' deterrence would refer to the conditions concerning the rightness of maintaining nuclear deterrence and the ways deterrence should be conducted. "If one side of the dilemma is how to apply the moral wisdom contained in the just war tradition to the case of contemporary war", is the succinct observation of Paul Ramsey, " the other side is that we cannot escape doing so."[3]

Moral problems are created by the necessity of having to maintain nuclear weapons for the sake of deterrence posture. Ambiguity is more confounded as stable deterrence is assumed to ensure continued non-use of nuclear weapons. On the problem of morality of nuclear deterrence, Walzer observes thus: "The reason for our acceptance of deterrence strategy, most people would say, is that preparing to kill, even threatening to kill, is not at all the same thing as killing. Indeed it is not but it is frighteningly close - else deterrence would not work ... and it is in the nature of the closeness that the moral problem lies."[4]

The very notion of *jus in bello* requires us to proscribe even the threat of use of nuclear weapons. Yet, there are bound to be circumstances, in self-defence, which necessitate the existence of this threat. It is here that we move out of the limits of justice to achieve or maintain justice and peace.[5]

---

3. Paul Ramsey, *The Just War: Force and Political Responsibility* (New York: Charles Scribner's Sons, 1980), p.184.
4. Michael Walzer, *Just and Unjust Wars: A Moral Argument with Historical Illustrations* (London: Allen Lane, 1977), p.270.
5. Ibid, p.282.

Counter-force and Counter-value Targeting

When the application of force behoves the transgression of boundaries set by the *jus in bello* concepts of proportionality and discrimination, it demands an examination whether the defence of a nation's interest by force is morally justified. This raises the problem of the nature of values, the threats against them and the means employed to defend them. It prompts us to analyse *jus ad bellum* ie the war decision.[6] A nation must be able to envision a war policy involving the use of nuclear weapons that can satisfy the tenets of, both, discrimination and proportionality and one which, within these limits, is sufficient to deter. Such a policy need not be declared but must be left to the adversary to work out himself.

The *in bello* norm of discrimination for counter-city attacks, whether they be offensive or in retaliation, is reinforced by the principle of proportionality. Once a counter-city warfare commences, both parties to the war are bound to cross the threshold of nuclear absorption. This in fact violates the criterion of 'reasonable hope of success'.

Hence it is, in fact, not enough that civilian deaths be unintended. There has to be proportionality between the civilian deaths and military purposes to be achieved.[7] Needless to say that it would be ideal if civilian deaths are avoided entirely. Put in a more crude sense, maybe the fear of civilian deaths beyond a proportion could itself be a deterer – for the good or for worse. The crucial distinction

---

6. This term is used by O'Brien. It is meant to emphasise the difference between *ad bellum* and *in bello,* which refers to 'warfighting' once the decision to go to war has been made. Refer to William V O'Brien's book, *The Conduct of Just and Limited War* (New York: Praeger, 1981).
7. Walzer, n.4, pp.276 - 277.

in the theory and practice of war is not between prohibited and accepted weapons but between prohibited and accepted targets. This creates problems well before one gets to the question of nuclear escalation. The same holds true regarding strategic counter-force attacks against homelands.

The interesting moral question now is – can there be a morally acceptable destruction through use of nuclear weapons? Some moral theorists condoned tactical and counter-force warfare as it seemed to meet the formal requirements of *jus in bello*. But the collateral damage caused by counter-force targeting, even by use of tactical nuclear weapons, would be massive and lethal enough to violate the limits of proportionality.

Commenting on the theories of limited war in Europe, Raymond Aron observed, "The disproportion between costs of such hostilities and the results they could achieve would be colossal."[8] In all cases one is still bound by the traditional interpretation of the principle of double-effect, to weigh the evil consequences which indirectly accompany the attacks against the good effects that flow from it.[9] Thus, on the basis of traditional double-effect analysis, the collateral damage indirectly intended provides no justification for the employment of nuclear weapons.

While the killing of the non-combatant is undoubtedly wrong, the application of the principle of proportionality to the principle of discrimination illustrates the truth of David Ross's idea that right and good are not synonymous.

8. Quoted in Walzer, n.4, p.227.

9. For a discussion of the dispute about the direct-indirect distinction in Catholic moral theology, read John R Connery, "Catholic Ethics: Has the Norm for Rule-Making Changed?", *Theological Studies*, 42 (1981), pp.232-250; Germain Grisez and Russell Shaw, *Beyond the New Morality* (Notre Dame, US: University of Notre Dame Press, 1974); Lisa Sowle Cahill, "Theology, Utilitarianism and Christian Ethics", *Theological Studies*, 42 (1981), pp.601-629.

One range of good ideas may be right in a particular case; one out of many evil options may in certain other circumstances be at least justifiable. We may not do evil, however, that good may come.[10]

Ramsey has focussed entirely on questions related to the moral use of force, *jus in bello,* and within this framework, made an explicit connection between the idea of non combatant immunity and the Christian love for neighbour. This proved to be a powerful argument in the context of religious ethical reflections during the late 1950s and 1960s, dominated as it was by the concept of love, as the uniquely Christian conscientious criterion. Ramsey argued that the Christian idea of love gives birth to a twin-born Just War theory, including both justification and limitation of the use of force.[11]

The principle of discrimination means that it is never moral to directly and intentionally attack non-combatants. In contrast to proportionality, which moves according to the utilitarian calculus of good versus evil, discrimination expresses a moral absolute. Unintended indirect harm is not forbidden by the principle of discrimination. What is regarded iniquitous is non-combatants being made the intended targets. Hence, as Ramsey observes, within the criteria of *jus in bello,* the principle of discrimination has 'normative priority'. "Whatever is wrong to do is wrong to threaten ... If counter-population warfare is murder, then counterpopulation deterrent threats are murderous."[12]

---

10. Finnis, *Fundamentals of Ethics* (Oxford: Clarendon Press, 1983), pp.109-112. It refers to the Pauline principle, ie ends never justify means.
11. Paul Ramsey, n.3 and *War and Christian Conscience* (Durham: Duke University Press, 1961).
12. Paul Ramsey, "A Political Ethics Context for Strategic Thinking", in Morton Kaplan, *Strategic Thinking and Its Moral Implications* (Chicago: University of Chicago Press, 1973). Also quoted in Walzer, n.4, p.273.

It must be noted that deterrence based on counter-force targeting puts the intent of harm where it justly belongs – on the enemy's combatant forces. In such strikes, the principle of proportionality provides the only moral limitation. Immorality lies in the threat itself, not in its present or even its likely consequence. Walzer has this to say: "... it is our own intentions that we have to worry about and the potential victims ... of those intentions."[13]

St Thomas Acquinas justified killings in self-defence, committed with public authority and for public good because life is a basic human right in defence of which we are entitled to use force. However, "lawful authority and just cause would be insufficient if the intention were not righteous; such intention would be influenced by the principle of proportionality."[14]

If the killing of those non-combatants whose activities contribute to the more deadly activities of combatants is justified the problem is to differentiate:-

(a) When a killing has occurred in self-defence.

(b) Who intentionally contributed to the helping of combatants, and who did it for the sake of earning a livelihood.[15]

In fact Rev Anthony Kenny points out that, "To claim that a counter-force strategy... does not involve an attack

13. Walzer, n.4, p.272.

14. Arthur Hockaday, " The Aim of Just Deterrence: Peace with Justice", in M McCall and Oliver Ramsbotham, *Just Deterrence: Morality and Deterrence in the Twenty First Century*(London, School of Peace Studies: University of Bradford, 1989), p.57.

15. R Wasserstrom, "War, Nuclear War. and Nuclear Deterrence: Some Conceptual and Moral Issues", in Hardin, *Nuclear Deterrence: Ethics and Strategy* (Chicago: University of Chicago Press, 1985), p. 21.

on civilian population is like claiming to be not responsible for the death of a friend, if one shoots a bullet to kill a mosquito perched on his throat."[16]

O'Brien has argued that proportionality is a more fundamental norm than non-combatant immunity. Hence counter-city strikes can be justified for one reason – selective strategic counter-value attacks carried out to "deter a continuation of antecedent selective counter-value attacks by the aggressor". He is able to say so by ignoring the dangers of escalation and the criterion of reasonable hope of success.[17] Even if the inevitability of escalation is doubtful, one needs to consider the risks – especially in relation to proportionality, discrimination and reasonable hope of success.[18]

The main dispute over whether strategic counter-force war-fighting strategies are less objectionable than counter-city strategies is the prudential military-political judgement about whether the limitation of nuclear war can indeed be predicted with any reasonable amount of confidence. This is where reasonable hope of success becomes the relevant moral norm.

In his attempt to make Just War possible in the modern age, Ramsey has defended the use of modern tactical nuclear weapons against invading armies and of strategic weapons against nuclear installations, convenient military bases and isolated economic objectives, though these targets too are purely conditionally permissible because of the rule of proportionality. He has maintained that the collateral civilian damage that would result from counter-force warfare in its maximum form would be sufficient to deter potential aggressors.[19]

---

16. Rev Anthony Kenny, quoted in Walter Stein (ed), *Nuclear Weapons and Christian Conscience* (London: Merlin Press,1961), p.162.
17. O'Brien comprehends the need to understand the importance of danger of escalation.
18. Richard Harries, *Christianity and War in the Nuclear Age* (London: Mowbray, 1986), p.66.
19. Ramsey, n.3, p.252.

For Ramsey, the non-combatants are the incidental victims of legitimate military strikes. Such warfare with such collateral damage is morally superior to deterrence. What is however ignored is that the threat of collateral damage is ineffective unless the damage is disproportionate to the objectives of war or the actual value of military targets. "The threat of something disproportionate", argues Ramsey, "is not always a disproportionate threat".[20]

Criticising Ramsey, Walzer stated that "given the effect it does have and the central part it is assigned, the word collateral seems to have lost much of its meaning. Surely anyone designing such a strategy must accept moral responsibility for the effects on which he is so radically dependent."[21]

Johnson warns of the need to be aware of the long-term effects of the weapons used. In view of the immoral outcomes of the nuclear attack, one can never overlook the fact that "after any war, all are non-combatants and the use of weapons that will endanger generations yet unborn by making target areas unlivably hot represents as much a violation of non-combatancy as a bullet through the brain of a child held hostage to cause an enemy to surrender." According to Johnson, it would be ideal to have weapons, which, if used, would have temporary effects "... that could be used in the contexts typical of war directly and intentionally against combatants while avoiding harm to non-combatants."[22]

Nevertheless, the intention to kill civilians under certain circumstances is omnipresent and, most probably, such a

20. Ibid, p.303.

21. Walzer, n.4, p.280.

22. James Turner Johnson, *Can Modern War be Just?* (New Haven, Conn: Yale University Press, 1984).

threat is a necessity in order to deter an aggressor who would not risk harm to his own civilians. However, in most cases it is the least-concerned leadership which orders a strike on another nation. In fact the very threat and preparedness for indiscriminate attack is against morality. And "...there are thousands of men trained in the techniques of mass destruction and drilled in instant obedience" standing ready to carry out orders. "And from the perspective of morality, the readiness is all."[23]

According to Johnson, foreseeable yet unavoidable harm to non-combatants in a battle area may be allowed in order to protect non-combatants in other geographic areas who would be harmed "or to protect values of equal or greater weight than harm to innocent persons by use of indiscriminate means of war."[24] Morally, this is the last resort.

It is in reality the presence of civilians that has either made leaders hesitate to declare their war intentions or else an attack has been deterred for fear of hurting them. But, the consideration for proportionality has always had priority over discrimination. Moreover, the principle of proportionality calls for lower total collateral destruction and an avoidance of high yield weapons with high circular error probability in counter-force attacks. It could also be said that such accuracy could be destabilising because of possible pressure of pre-emption. The issue of first use of nuclear weapons in a conflict poses afresh the dilemma of assessing a threat as against its execution in moral terms. A first-use represents the breaching of a threshold and erodes the very value of distinction between use of nuclear weapons and non-nuclear weapons. As Garfinkle states: "There is in fact an inverse relationship between raising

23. Walzer, n.4, p.272.
24. Johnson, n.22.

the nuclear threshold and raising threshold of outbreak of war in general, but a direct relationship between credibility of deterrence and the prospect of nuclear war."[25] "To declare an intention first", adds Garfinkle, "to employ nuclear weapons as a conscious act of national policy is to threaten to become involved in a process which will ultimately lead to use of these weapons by choice and not by mindless escalation."[26]

Such an outcome is bound to prompt the deterred state to base its own strategy on the early use of nuclear weapons. Deterrence, after all, does not express an absolute intention not to use nuclear weapons. It in fact expresses a conditional intention to use them, in certain circumstances. If deterrence never implied such an intention, it would hardly be effective. It requires at least the "remotest of possibilities" to be credible and even this minimum is enough to disallow any separation between deterrence and use.

On the other hand, if the nuclear threshold is lowered by having more plausibly usable weapons (accurate with low yield) the risk of a nuclear war is reduced. But then the chances of any war escalating to a nuclear war are great. If, on the contrary, having only counter-value weapons raises the nuclear threshold (inaccurate with high yield) the chances of a war for lesser stakes than necessary are increased; but then there is less likelihood of a nuclear war.

There is no conditional intention to use nuclear weapons, writes Bruce Kent. He has this to say: "The willingness to use nuclear weapons is a present reality on a daily basis for those in the armed forces who have responsibility for them...Nor is

25. Adam Garfinkle, "The Attack on Deterrence: Reflections on Morality and Strategic Praxis", *Journal of Strategic Studies* (June 1989), p.175.
26. Ibid.

there any way in which our present strategic nuclear weapons can be used discriminatingly even if limited war were actually possible and the genetic change in the future generations ignored...the more accurate they become the more they will be seen as weapons of preemptive first strike and the more unstable the situation becomes."[27] For Johnson, however, it is not that just cause inevitably takes priority over just restrained conduct of war but rather that a balance must be kept between considerations to use force and how to use it. For this, it is essential that the firebreak between nuclear and conventional weapons be wide and strong. Such dilemmas are related to the basic norms observed by a society and sought to be protected by its decision makers. To recognise them and sort them according to priorities (though each society would have different priorities among the same set of values) is an art learnt in a community of moral discourse.[28]

The weight of each value will become apparent when threatened or violated. All depends on the nature of those values and the interrelation among them because the utility of one value conflicts with that of the other. It would be very difficult to demarcate between values on a priority basis.

The problems of morality and nuclear weapons are more confounded when we ask how good are the values to be defended? Can values be defended by forceful means? For Walzer, the justification for fighting lies in recognition of evil and revolting against it.[29] The root cause of threat to

---

27. Bruce Kent, "A Christian Utilitarianism from a Christian Background", in Geoffrey Goodwin, ed, *Ethics and Nuclear Deterrence* (London: Croom Helm, 1981), p.65.
28. James Turner Johnson, "On Keeping Faith: The Uses of History for Religious Ethics", *The Journal of Religious Ethics*, 7 (Spring 1979), pp.98-116, at p.103.
29. Walzer, n.4. The values endangered are those of justice, freedom, independence, which are important for personal dignity and a nation's integrity.

these values come from an excessive diversion of resources to military enhancement, especially for a nuclear overkill capacity. The distinguished theologian John Courtney Murray says: "It is not enough simply to consider the sorrows and evils that flow from war. There are greater evils than the physical death and destruction wrought in war. And there are human goods of so high an order that immense sacrifices may have to be borne in their defense."[30]

This is also the fundamental rationale of Just War tradition, a position that makes it all the more necessary to think about how to structure military doctrine as well as the aspect of deployment of weapons to be used in an armed conflict. It is sometimes suggested that more lethal the weapons the more the chances that it can shorten the duration of conflict, thereby reducing the misery of those involved in it. After all, "What is wrong ... is not the desire to shorten armed conflicts when they do break out ; it is the assumption that is the chief goal to be served."[31] The issue is to hold the use of military force within moral limits. The political ideals, which such force serves are themselves framed in morally justifiable terms and the means of war are in principle capable of being kept under the control of moral intentionality.[32]

There is need to emphasise limitation, relativity and control. Johnson provides a justification for weapons that could be brought within the criterion of use of force

30. J C Murray, *We Hold These Truths : Catholic Reflections on the American Proposition* (New York : Sheed & Ward, 1960), p. 261.

31. Johnson, n.22, p.112. Also see Leonard Cheshire, *The Light of Many Suns* (London : Methuen, 1985).

32. Johnson, n.22.

within the Just War limitations of proportionality and discrimination.[33] He considers the neutron warhead to be within the parameters because it is not a pure radiation weapon by any means but a miniaturised fusion warhead with effects characteristic of larger strategic warheads, though proportionally smaller. Neutron radiation is enhanced but not long-enduring. From the standpoint of discrimination, it has an advantage over tactical fission and high explosive warheads which it displaces.[34] What distinguishes the neutron warhead is its smaller long-term effect : less property damage and less long-term residual radiation. It exploits radiation effect as compared with blast and heat. The level of damage would be less than from the fission and thermonuclear weapons. The effect on military personnel is expected to be as great as of any other weapon. Johnson further states that if account were to be taken of the total effect on the belligerent populations, in particular on those people whose homes and livelihoods are found in combat areas, the new weapon emerges as possibly a more proportionate means of waging modern war.[35]

Johnson propounds a general criterion for the employment of weapons: "... the most discriminating and proportional weapons should be those of first resort, while the least discriminating and proportional should be those last chosen".[36]

Johnson also maintains that the accuracy of cruise missiles and the variety of types of warheads available mark these weapons as falling within the criteria of weapons

33. Ibid, Chapter 5.
34. Ibid, p.115.
35. Ibid, p.117.
36. Ibid.

that could be justifiably and legitimately used. Cruise missiles allow for change in direction of missiles in flight and "homing in" on the most vital part of a target by corrections of course close to time of impact, with controllability depending on the efficacy of the guidance mechanism.

Apart from being cheaper and having potential for avoiding detection in flight, this accuracy makes it suitable to adopt a defence strategy oriented principally around the concept of counter-force warfare.[37]

(a) High yield strategic nuclear warheads. The fact is that when a target is close to a population centre, the very power of strategic warheads would destroy the non-combatant areas nearby. Fewer strategic warheads may be needed to destroy a military target; hence the lowered destruction of non-combatant areas.

(b) Low yield tactical nuclear warheads. The delivery systems of such warheads are precise and difficult to defend against. One disadvantage of cruise missiles is that, if deployed for tactical use, they could "extend the theatres of operations and raise the level of destruction to combatants and non-combatants alike.[38] The accuracy to target the intended areas necessitates the lowering of number of warheads required. A lower yield warhead does the job of a high yield warhead.

(c) Conventional high-explosive warheads. The capability to discriminate among targets at long-range has opened the possibility of replacing nuclear warheads with those of conventional high explosives for tactical and even strategic use.

37. Ibid. pp.124-125.

38. Ibid, p. 126.

Johnson, justifying these weapons on the grounds of being within the permitted limits, states that the low cost, accuracy, ability to penetrate defences, easy utility in combat and possibility of deploying them with conventional warheads makes cruise missiles more attractive to have in the defence arsenal.

The idea is to develop more manageable, more discriminating and more proportionate weapons for use in situations where forces are genuinely necessary. Discriminate use requires accuracy and some targets may have to be foregone.

Johnson refers to the decapitation strategy, which involves much more selective targeting. The targets are command, control and communications network of the military and political forces of a potential enemy. The main criterion for judging this is to be within the moral purview of discrimination and proportionality. Here is a principle of "economy of force ... carried to a new high level".[39] The three principles, economy of force, proportionality and discrimination, converge. For Johnson, it is from this convergence that decapitation strategy appears morally to be a worthwhile idea. "The principle involved is the same one established classically in international law that makes rulers liable for wars waged at their behest". Johnson concedes that this principle suggests political assassination at the extreme as the most discriminate and proportionate means of war though the moral question arises because of the difficulty to distinguish between assassination and murder.[40]

Aware of the fact that nuclear weapons are both indiscriminate and disproportionate, Johnson has attempted to fit accurate and low yield warheads and delivery systems

---

39. Ibid, p. 144.
40. Ibid, pp. 145-146.

"in the service of a morally informed human intentionality". This advantage has led Johnson to sanction, however, grudgingly, precisely those weapons and strategies, which from the nuclear arms control perspective, have been the most destabilising and prone to pre-emptive strike. The neutron warhead, the cruise missile, the MX missile — it was around these technological innovations that the massive peace movement gained momentum. Counter-force targeting accelerated the nuclear arms race. David Allen Rosenberg has documented this fact. Nuclear decapitation strategy was condemned by arms control experts as a dangerous development. This as well as the effort to fit some weapons into the framework of the Just War tradition led to a paradoxical situation – even those who supported nuclear deterrence as well as conscientious objectors to it found these the most dangerous weapons and strategies. In their view, they become part of nuclear war-fighting scheme.

II

Nuclear Deterrence and the Pastoral Letter of the American Catholic Bishops

Three types of justified war are identified in the Hebrew scriptures: war commanded by God; defensive war and war initiated by the King for his own purposes. Roman law required the authoritative publishing of the causes of war and a formal declaration that a state of war existed.

International law in the 20th century has gradually reduced the justification of war to defence. Defence refers to not only the prevention of injury (the Roman and Medieval term) but also the reaction to aggression already begun or completed. For Pope Pius aggression was not a moral option. Pope John XXIII ruled out retaliation against an aggression already accomplished. John's successor, Pope Paul VI expressed his views in just three words: "Never again war" – reminiscent of the Kellogg Briand Pact of 1928.

The problem of nuclear weapons is a human problem. Approximately five million people demonstrated in the West European capitals in the Autumn of 1981 and 1983.[41] For once people have the power to reverse God's creation, with weapons million times the power of the atom bomb that obliterated Hiroshima and Nagasaki, positioned on delivery systems and otherwise, that could be launched by intent or miscalculation.[42] The American Catholic Bishops were motivated by such a concern and for the first time "a deeply conservative hierarchy traditionally identified with patriotic sentiment and military strength took a firm position in opposition to the declared nuclear strategy of the United States."[43]

The Bishops explained that their intrusion into a subject far away from their pastoral duties – nuclear strategy – was due to an exceptional development in human progress. "We are the first generation since Genesis with the power to threaten the created order. We cannot remain silent in the face of such danger".[44]

They had the courage to address the gravest moral problem well aware that whatever they said would be open to criticism, especially if it were contrary to the American defence policy. This did not deter them, said Cardinal Joseph Bernadin, the leader of the drafting group : "Silence in this instance would be a betrayal of its (Church's) mission

---

41. Mary Kaldor, "After the Cold War", *New Left Review* (March-April 1990), No. 80, p.34.
42. Foreword by Theodore M Hesburgh, in Philip J Murnion (ed), *Catholics and Nuclear War: A Commentary on the Challenge of Peace: The US Catholic Bishop's Pastoral Letter on War and Peace* (New York: Crossroad, 1983), p.xii.
43. E P Thompson, *Star Wars* (Harmondsworth : Penguin Books, 1985), p.244.
44. "The Challenge of Peace : God's Promise and Our Response", *Strategic Digest* (November 1983), pp.691-745, at 694.

... Nuclear weapons and nuclear strategy constitute a qualitatively new moral problem."[45] The Pastoral Letter "ambushed President Reagan from an unexpected quarter ... He had supposed that he was the nations's specialist in moral homilies, but here were competitors who could threaten the sovereignty over the world He had brought into being and who could destroy His work".[46]

As a noted mathematical physicist has admitted, scientists had written a great deal about nuclear strategy "but nothing we have written is as thoughtful as the Pastoral Letter on War and Peace ... that letter is indeed a challenge to us scientists as well as to everybody else".[47]

The Drafting of the Letter

The letter is admirable for the fact that in their field of reference there are no theological or moral precedents. The drafting process was open – something unusual in the production of Church documents. It involved scientists, theologians, specialists in nuclear theory and strategy and those who in general agreed and disagreed with the direction in which the document was going. The Ad Hoc Committee on War and Peace, established in 1981, chaired by Cardinal Joseph Bernadin of Cincinati, included Bishops George Fulcher, Daniel Reilly, Thomas Gumbleton; the President of Pax Christi, Bishop John O'Connor – Second in Command of the Catholic Military Chaplains, monks and nuns from other religious groups, Father Bryan Hehir, Director of the Conference's Department of International Peace and Justice in Washington DC, Edward Dougherty

45. Thompson, n.43, p.25.

46. n.2.

47. Freeman Dyson, *Infinite in All Directions* (New York: Harper & Row, 1988 / Perennial Library edn, 1989), p.24.

of the same office, a retired US Foreign Service Officer and Bruce M Russett of Yale University as the 'principal consultant'.[48]

The Committee proceeded with many days of discussions and hearings at which about fifty experts were heard and questioned. Concerned about the impact of any criticism directed at American nuclear strategy, the Reagan Administration sent senior officials to reassure the Bishops that American official policy strictly adhered to the principle of discrimination.

After circulation and criticism of various portions, the Committee's first draft of the letter was released early in June of 1982. It became the subject of widespread discussion. Thousands of pages were submitted commenting on the draft. After scrupulously studying the defence provided by the Reagan Administration, they declared that no defence can be made for the destruction of the Soviet cities.[49] In the final debate, a rationale-laced condemnation was given: "Such a strike would be deemed morally disproportionate even though not intentionally indiscriminate." It held out the possibility of a tolerable nuclear attack on isolated but significant conventional units proving the desperate grip that a limited nuclear war had on the claim of moral respectability.

The proposed forbearance of the counter-force nuclear strategy was the target of criticism. In October, when the second draft appeared, the passage on counter-force had been entirely deleted and there appeared the unequivocal condemnation of

48. Bruce Russett, "The Statement of American Catholic Bishops : A Moral Theological Critique of Nuclear Deterrence", *Bulletin of Peace Proposals*, Vol.15, No.3 (1984).

49. Albert Carnesale, et.al., *Living With Nuclear Weapons* (New York : Bantam Books, 1983), pp.117-118.

any use of nuclear weapons in a war.[50] The reason was that the experts were unsure how to control a nuclear war. They knew how to start a war not how to end one. The third draft was released in April and became subject to the formal process of amendment. On May 3, 1983, 247 Bishops assembled for the voting of the final text. After hundreds of amendments in the three-month process, the letter as amended was adopted by a vote of 328 to. 9, i.e. 96% in favour.

The letter elicited great public attention to the issues of nuclear weaponry and established those issues not as "esoterically technical issues best left to the 'priesthood' of civilian and military strategies" but as fundamentally political and moral issues which were indeed the responsibility of ordinary citizens. This is the letter's most enduring achievement.

The Letter

The Bishops began their discussion on the fundamental principles of morality. Nuclear weapons were not acceptable as a permanent feature of international security, not only because they expose the people to unacceptable dangers but even more because there is an inherent intention, under certain conditions, to commit unacceptable crimes.[51] Three aspects of nuclear deployment were condemned by them – deliberate targeting of civilian population, willingness to use nuclear weapons first under certain circumstances and planning to fight limited nuclear wars. The consensus was forged around the long established tradition of Just War. This provided the standards through which states are justified in waging a war : the cause must be just; authority legitimate and resort to force a last resort. It was presented as a legitimate choice. The Bishops,

50. Francis X Winters, "Did the Bishops Ban the Bomb : Yes and No", *America*, Vol. 149, No.6 (September 1983), pp.104-108, at p.105.
51. Dyson, n.47.

however, took care not to prescribe non-violence. They believed in all sincerity in the right of self-defence and that there are major values – liberty, justice, human rights – to be defended.

Even though military installations or industries might themselves be permissible targets, the good to be achieved (or evil prevented by hitting them) would have to be some way balanced against the harm done in killing innocent civilians, indirectly or unintentionally. This principle, therefore, leads to great scepticism about whether even a 'limited' use of nuclear weapons could be justified. It is also confounded by doubts that command and control capabilities are, or could ever be, adequate to contain the use of those weapons at sufficiently limited levels.

The letter is a complex blend of issues scriptural, ethical, political and strategic. Their Just War premises, their evidence and their logic, taken together, drive so strongly towards absolute nuclear pacifist conclusions that their reasons for the moral acceptance of nuclear deterrence must lie elsewhere than in the thrust of their arguments.

A strong adherence to a moral equivalence of intention and action implied that 'deterrent intentions' were exempt from all such moral equivalence because of their peculiarly positive consequences of the intention per se.[52] A moral equivalence of intention and action meant that the only deterrent threats that are acceptable are the threats to use nuclear weapons in ways and circumstances that could be morally acceptable. However, the Just War criteria and other controlling factors that the Bishops consider necessary for any deterrent policy that is to be even temporarily acceptable to

52. Gregory Kavka, "Some Paradoxes of Deterrence", *The Journal of Philosophy*, 75 (June 1978), pp.285-302.

them make it extremely doubtful that any effective policy of nuclear deterrence could meet their standards.[53]

On the Use of Nuclear Weapons

The Bishops were careful, however, not to advocate unilateral disarmament. They recognised, reluctantly though, the moral justification for the possession of nuclear weapons solely as a deterrent to nuclear war. But this permissible retention of nuclear weapons was subjected to severe limitations. First, the weapons could only be used in retaliation after a nuclear attack. Second, if they were not to reject nuclear deterrence absolutely, the Bishops had to find some tactics that at least had a possibility, in some hypothetical circumstances, of being morally neutral rather than intrinsically evil. This was, thus, 'a strictly conditioned acceptance' of nuclear weapons. The temporary acceptance of the possession of nuclear weapons was to be coupled with serious efforts to achieve disarmament. "We do not perceive any situation in which the deliberate initiation of nuclear warfare, on however, restricted a scale can be morally justified", they stated.[54] Interestingly, since neither the Pope nor the Vatican Council had condemned all possible uses of nuclear weapons, it was not, given the hierarchical nature of the Church, open to the American Bishops to do so. The ambiguity in the Pastoral Letter was in some way to accommodate the views of the more nuclear pacifist Bishops who would not have tolerated any statement about the legitimacy of nuclear deterrence.

The Bishops were extremely sceptical of whether the use of nuclear weapons would possibly pass the tests of

53. Susan Moller Okin, "The Moral Acceptability of Nuclear Deterrence: A Critique", *Politics*, Vol.18 (November 1983), pp.527-554, at pp. 528-531.

54. Russett, n.48, p.203.

discrimination, proportionality and reasonable chance of success. They were aware of the risks of escalation even in the best of circumstances and, if the opponent were to begin a war, some of those risks would already have been taken. To deter the same and bring the war to a negotiated halt, a restricted plan of retaliation was permitted, but the risk of first use was too high to justify such an action. As they said : "We have no experience of control, much testimony against its possibility and, therefore, no moral justification for submitting the human community to this risk".[55]

They expressed their "profound scepticism about the moral acceptability of any use of nuclear weapons". They were against the use of nuclear weapons whether they be against civilian centres of population or against military targets, whether in a first strike or in a retaliatory second strike. Their rejection of even a limited nuclear war was complete.

They made a binding and clear cut statement regarding the use of nuclear weapons on non-combatants or the harm it would cause them, using the principle of discrimination, which happens to be the most controversial criteria of Just War. "Under no circumstances may nuclear weapons or other instruments of mass slaughter be used for the purpose of destroying population centres of the predominantly civilian targets."[56]

Attempts to search for a median between total rejection of nuclear deterrence due to its inescapable implications for innocent civilians and the seeming seal of approval of the hazards of counter-force strategies is delicate. It is over these impediments that some of the

55. Ibid.

56. The Challenge of Peace, n.44, p.693.

most remarked-about changes in the letter occurred. Ambiguity had to be removed in the third draft and the form finally adopted at the Chicago meeting.

The Bishops called for 'sufficiency' and rejected any quest for nuclear superiority. They opposed any proposals that had or would have the effect of lowering the nuclear threshold and blurring the difference between nuclear and conventional weapons (probably including the neutron bomb). Furthermore, they recommended a variety of measures including a comprehensive test ban treaty, removal of nuclear weapons from the border areas where they could be overrun in war (thus forcing early decision on their use), and immediate, bilateral and verifiable agreements to halt the testing, production and deployment of new nuclear weapon systems. This last was widely, and correctly, perceived as meaning support for a freeze.

Perhaps the substructure of their efforts to avoid endorsing a limited nuclear war was their advocacy of a policy of no first use of nuclear weapons. It is not quite an unequivocal rejection of first-use. "We do not perceive any situation in which the deliberate initiation of nuclear warfare, on however, restricted a scale, can be morally justified". But it came very close to it. In doing so the Bishops rejected the idea of using nuclear weapons for 'extended deterrence' and required that non-nuclear attacks be resisted by other than nuclear means. The risks of first use of nuclear weapons were, according to them, too high to justify ever setting the process into motion.

On Deterrence

The Bishops' letter is the epitome of their puzzled conscience. They balanced their decisive 'no' to nuclear war with a qualified 'yes' to the strategy of deterrence. Perhaps it was the fear that nuclear weapons would undoubtedly be used in violation of a "no first use". They, of course, realised that an un-reciprocated reduction would remove the one leverage that the West had to reduce the Soviet arsenal, which would create a destablising situation in the international, especially West European, politics. In this environment of struggle between conscience and consequent confusion, they were comforted by the reassuring words of Pope John Paul II, when he indicated that deterrence was not intolerable, 'for the time being'. 'Nothing less guarantees security and nothing more satisfies conscience'.

They were willing to consider some strengthening of conventional defence 'as a proportionate price to pay' if it would reduce the possibility of a nuclear war. Appreciative of Europe's astonishing political and economic recovery from the last War, they did not believe that Europe could not be defended by other than nuclear weapons. They were, however, not too confident of the deterring capabilities of conventional weapons. The hurdles were political rather than economic or military, and basically because of a lack of political will.

The Bishops hoped that the good effect would not have to depend upon the evil one. A choice had to be made intending only the good effect while tolerating the evil one. The good effect of continuing to maintain the arsenal is political and the other effect is the military one. On this basis, inert arsenal was regarded as a moral option. However, the Bishops pondered on the politico-military question of how an effective deterrence could be maintained on the mere "physical capacity inherent in the nuclear arsenal, when national policy (was) opposed to its use."[57] They concluded that deterrence was in the eye of the beholder.[58] It is the arsenal that the Soviet planner would look to not the declaratory policy. They seem to have struggled

57. Ramsey, n.3., pp. 302-305 and Thomas Schelling, *Arms and Influence* (New Haven : Yale University Press, 1961), pp. 39-40.
58. Charles Krauthammer, "On Nuclear Morality", *Commentary* 76 (April 1983), p.49.

over the language they used for deterrence. They have provided a 'just war' analysis of deterrence that many people will use to say that nuclear weapons are in fact per se evil. The effect of this analysis is to demonstrate that the traditional Just War teaching is in fact alive and well. It is nuclear deterrence that does not look so healthy.

The Bishops' premises led them to conclude that while the need for military deterrence could not be evaded in a "conflicting world of states", relatively lower levels of threat were adequate and a shift to lower levels was required. This meant a no city-busting and no first strike capability, and the extended deterrence of conventional attack can succeed without reliance on nuclear threats. A shift to lower levels was required because of the ever-present chance that deterrence may fail.

Finally, the Bishops stated that deterrence, however defined, can only be an interim strategy on the road to disarmament. The Bishops had begun by strongly condemning the mass slaughter of civilians that the use of nuclear weapons entails but finally gave their "strictly conditional" acceptance of nuclear deterrence as an interim remedy while nuclear disarmament was being worked out. Some have argued that the Bishops' critique permits the bare possibility of the most restricted use of nuclear weapons. But the Bishops' position could not be reconciled with the official American deterrent posture.[59] They called for using the 'peace of a sort' as the framework to move towards authentic peace through nuclear arms control, reduction and disarmament, aware of the time-consuming process of moving from a nuclear to a non-nuclear defensive strategy. The relation between maintenance of a

59. B Russett, "Ethical Dilemmas of Nuclear Deterrence", *International Security* (Spring 1984), pp.52-53.

credible deterrent and the reduction of the military capacity has proven to be the Achille's heel for every arms reduction proposal since World War II: the Bishops' Letter is certainly not a final word on technical and political problems. They have grappled with this issue but they have not been able to resolve them.

The Bishops presented a far better case against the moral acceptability of deterrence than the case in its favour.[60] Despite their rejection of a completely pacifist position their logic and the weight of their evidence lead them to the same conclusion. Their argument that the nuclear strike is as immoral as the nuclear threat seems to have been directed at intellects like Paul Ramsey whose moral defence of counter-force deterrence relies heavily on the distinction between intentional and unintentional harm that the Bishops term as "perverted moral casuistry".[61] They rejected the targeting plans but the thrust of their arguments was blunted to suit the members of the military. (For example, they prohibited harm to innocent civilians but bless the Catholics in armed forces). They neither leave the problem nor are they able to fully confront this problem. They in fact seemed to have also sensed clearly the danger of engaging in specifying the ideal counter-force deterrence strategy that would be acceptable to them.[62] In fact counter-force strategy aided by technological advances escalates arms race to a point of no limit.[63] As Barnet has observed, nuclear force is regarded as "flexible" for achieving purposes

60. Okin, n.53, pp.16-26.
61. Ramsey, n.3, pp.302-305.
62. Jim Castelli, *The Bishops and the Bomb : Waging Peace in a Nuclear Age* (New York : Doubleday, 1983), pp.181-182.
63. Barry R Posen & Stephen Van Evera, "Defence Policy and the Reagan Administration : Departure From Containment", *International Security* 8 (Summer 1983), pp.3-45 at pp.12-14.

other than deterrence, and the arms race becomes a never-ending escalating contest.[64]

The Bishops' conditional acceptance of nuclear deterrence left them in a seriously paradoxical situation. They could not condone counter-force deterrence because if executed, it would involve massive civilian damage, though indirectly. They were left with the only deterrence that is most dangerous of all – deterrence based on the threat to disable the adversary's strategic nuclear capability. This meant making one's own weapons invulnerable.[65] But just as technology helps to achieve this, it also provides methods for rendering this invulnerability vulnerable. Even the theory of Just War seems to belong to the "domain of personal morality" and the concept of justice within which it works is more individualistic than political. Pope John Paul II provided a very valid observation when he says: "... together with the will for peace that all profess and that most desire, there is also in existence, perhaps in latent or conditional form, but nonetheless real, the contrary and the negation of this will, taking the risk that sometime, somewhere, somehow, someone can set in motion the terrible mechanism of general destruction".[66]

In *Pacem in Terris,* Pope John XXIII said that: "In this age which boasts of atomic power, it no longer makes sense to maintain that war is a fit instrument with which to repair the

---

64. Richard Barnet, "Reporter at Large: The Search for National Security", *The New Yorker* (April 27, 1981), p.62.
65. Stanley R Sloan & Robert G Gray, *Nuclear Strategy and Arms Control* (New York: Foreign Policy Association), Headline Series, No. 261 (November 1982), pp.41-42.
66. Bishop John J O Connor, "The Church's View on Nuclear Arms", in Earnest W Lefever, & Stephen E Hunt (ed), *The Apocalyptic Premise: Nuclear Arms Debated* (Washington D.C. : Ethics and Public Policy Centre, 1982), pp. 299-300.

violation of justice". This, as has been mentioned earlier, is the essence of the Letter. But then, instead of outright rejection of nuclear weapons we note that the Bishops have said, "As long as the danger of war remains, there is no competent and sufficiently powerful authority at international level, governments can not be denied the right to legitimate self-defence, once every means of settlement have been exhausted". True, this statement cannot be challenged, but is legitimate defence possible with nuclear weapons, whatever the urgency?

The Bishops' efforts to tackle the ethical dilemmas of nuclear deterrence is commendable. Hundreds of Church leaders grappled for more than two years under some measure of collective discipline (despite the problems of having to work under the Church hierarchy and the need to keep in mind not to go against the interests of the administration) to develop and perfect what the authors called "a teleology of peace suited to a civilisation poised on the brick of destruction." Influenced by this extraordinary Letter on War and Peace, the Christian groups and Churches of other nations – France, Netherlands and the two Germanys[67] – joined in the efforts to contribute their share in the common outcry against reliance on nuclear weapons. Machiavelli had believed that a good Christian had no business in politics.[68] But the Letter provided the much needed moral basis to political decisions.

67. Jean Klein, "The French Church and Current Problems of Peace and War : An Evolving Debate", pp. 219-225 ; Thomas Risse-Kappen, "Final Respite or Unconditional No : The Church and the Question of Peace in the FRG", pp. 205-212 ; Joachim Garstecki, "Peace Work Within the Church in GDR : Taking an Ethical Stand on Conditions of 'Real Socalisms'", pp. 213-218; Philip P Everts, "The Churches and Attitudes on Nuclear Weapons: The Case of the Netherlands", pp. 227-242 in *Bulletin of Peace Proposals,* Vol. 15, No.3 (1984).

68. Machiavelli, *The Prince* quoted in Adam Garfinkle, "The Attack on Deterrence: Reflections on Morality and Strategic Praxis", *The Journal of Strategic Studies* (June 1989), pp. 166-199, at p.190.

5

Reflections

I

In the post-World War II international politics, deterrence – in theory and practice – was considered as a sufficing solution in response to the requirements of security and preventing a war. It sounded, as Lawrence Freedman says, robust without being reckless. Forces were used only to contain the enemy, not to compel a change in the status quo.[1] The Cold War actors practiced restraint by ensuring that their threat of annihilation was believed by the adversary to be credible, controlling in the process the incentives to initiate a war. Inventions and innovations in weapon technology were essential to sustain this threat; and political equilibrium was attained.

Despite a sense of optimism that a political solution to conflicting environment was nearer at hand, the trust in deterrence was so much that it could not be done away with – the unknown risk-perception of the deterred based on the knowledge that nuclear weapons were as yet not obsolete. The Kremlin still had large nuclear arsenal. Russia, though no longer

1. L Freedman, "Does Deterrence Have a Future?", *Arms Control Today* (October 2000), pp.3-8, at p.3.

the awesome enemy, had problems around its borders. The former Soviet Union had a gradually dying military and an unmanageable rebellion in Chechnya to cope with. NATO witnessed many of the former Warsaw members coming into its fold. The ruthless policy adopted in Yugoslavia and Iraq made Russia sit up to this new form of international relations and maintenance of 'peace'. Viewing the eastward expansion of NATO and still unsure of the West's intentions, the Russians took shelter under the umbrella of nuclear deterrence.[2]

Deterrence was, thus, maintained while nuclear inventory was cut and reorganised. The "destabilising" elements of the strategic nuclear arsenal, the MIRVed and the ICBMs were cut back with submarine launched missiles, both ballistic and cruise, retaining their role. Short range "tactical" weapons were no longer carried at sea. A nuclear equivalent to all conventional munitions was no longer sought.[3] Nuclear posture had been placed on low key and deterrence was given a new meaning. With military technology advancing far ahead, the search to device elaborate rationales for a doctrine of nuclear first use and the need to prove it as credible reduced. Ironically, this has given the potential threateners time to pause and consider the consequences of use of weapons of mass destruction (WMD) on the West.[4]

Some foes in the future, it is surmised, may be deterred by threats to their counter-value targets, requiring few, if any, US nuclear weapons. Other foes, highly motivated and notably cost and risk tolerant, may be deterred only by severe threats to many types of targets, requiring significant US nuclear capabilities.[5]

---

2. Ibid, p.6.
3. Ibid, p.5.
4. Daniel Gouré, "Nuclear Deterrence, Then and Now", *Policy Review* Online http://www.policyreview.org/dec02/goure.html.
5. Charles Krauthammer, "The Obsolescence of Deterrence" *The Weekly Standard,* http://www.theweeklystandard.com/default.asp).

The first Bush administration began the process of altering the size and posture of American nuclear forces – in cooperation with President Boris Yeltsin's regime in Russia – by detargeting US ballistic missiles, removing nuclear weapons from strategic bombers, withdrawing almost all tactical nuclear weapons from forward positions, and agreeing to the START II treaty that promised to reduce the number of available nuclear weapons in the force to 3,500. The Clinton administration pursued implementation of these decisions as well as a variety of so-called threat reduction measures designed primarily to reduce risks associated with the arsenal of the former Soviet Union.[6]

II

Nuclear weapons will continue to play a role in the strategic calculations of the US and Russia. The shift in American attitude towards deterrence could be seen in the debates over missile defence over the years. In case America goes on to justify its hegemonic cause more than once the more it would see the other countries making alliances against American justification of attacks on any country. Traditional deterrence is no guide when it comes to assessing nuclear plans as far as the West or Russia is concerned. For the new nuclear states, they get to learn from the pros and cons of the history of the Cold War and plan their own version of deterrence. Each nation is bound to take a different approach to the development of its military doctrine conditioned by its opponents, experiences in war and other military experiences. In fact, in the contemporary period, individual, diplomatic and military moves are justified on their own terms rather than on the terms of deterrence. Deterrence is tried to be played down and yet it is required to explain why certain strategic moves are foreclosed or why other moves are

---

6. Daniel Gouré, n.4.

regarded as essential. Even today it makes sense to use deterrence as a policy to make states aware that if a line is crossed it would entail a forceful response.

Critics are never worn down pointing out the fallacy of such a policy. The threat needs force, which implies credibility. Deterrence is a way to control behaviour of states and providing a warning against a breach of conduct that is detrimental to the interests of a country or the world in general. Deterrence is a strategy, which does not state explicitly the outcome of that breach.

One needs to note the other side of the story also. Apart from the mindset of deterrence being a success story, there are cases where this may not be so. The gap between what the deterring nation feels is an adequate or correct policy to deter another nation, and what in actuality is the target nation's decision maker's actual criterion, is also a deciding factor. Thus, a nation must be prepared not only to execute deterrence but also be prepared to accept that deterrence may not always work. In that eventuality, the nation must be prepared with suitable forces to defeat and/or punish aggression. Where an aggressor executes an action so rapidly that it seems more of a challenge thrown at the victim nation, it would surely result in a costly response.

Bernard Brodie maintained that with the inclusion of strategic nuclear weapons, strategic bombing should be the ultimate form of war. Standing against preventive war, pre-emptive strike and massive retaliation, Brodie argued that a US retaliatory force should be ready as deterrence could not be workable on every occasion. He drew attention to nuclear deterrence in his structural analysis of deterrence, and he stressed the danger of being unable to predict one's own behaviour in a crisis.[7]

---

7. Ken Booth, "Bernard Brodie", in John Baylis and John Garnett, (eds.), *Makers of Nuclear Strategy* (London : Pinter 1991), pp. 34-35.

III

To surmise the intangible forces requires vision. The options and the design of deterrence have changed. Expecting the probable response of the opponent is near impossible. Containment is history. For, the future will undoubtedly bring in conflicts that are different and surprising, ensuring little or no opportunity for developing standard approaches to them. Wisely observed is the statement that one will have to note the fine difference between that which is rational and that which is reasonable behavior. To assume rationality and on that basis to expect behavior that is reasonable – that is behavior predictably driven by familiar, understandable norms and goals is to risk lethal surprise.[8]

The use of 'deterrence' is yet to fade into history and the enemy is unconventional. The situation remains one where nations are threatened by the unseen enemy who could threaten or use nuclear, biological or chemical weapons to have their way against a state. These weapons have become a great deal more common and their numbers have increased, along with their firepower. Policies, thus, have to be more flexible. There is bound to be a want of the same level of confidence, or more, in dealing with certain new nuclear states and new threats.

A matter of worry is the general attitude towards ensuring against risks of malfunction, breach of security of weapons, accidents or thefts, the stress and strain of low resources and low morale that is bound to take its toll on the security of the nuclear weapons and material that is stored. This, ironically, makes the Russian deterrent strong because in case of any crisis the West would have to show stronger restraint – the disaster could be a result of inadvertence not deliberation.

8. Keith B Payne, "The Fallacies of Cold War Deterrence and a New Direction", *Comparative Strategy* 22 (2003), pp. 411-428, at p. 412.

Nuclear accident, or even the deliberate use of nuclear weapons through the third force – the anti state groups – cannot be ruled out.

The Bush and Clinton administrations were reluctant to seriously challenge the nuclear doctrines of the Cold War. Both were concerned that Russia's political transformation might not succeed, resulting in the emergence of a hostile power. In its 1994 Nuclear Posture Review and a 1997 Presidential Decision Directive, the Clinton administration maintained a classic view of the role of nuclear weapons as a means of deterring war. To that end, the United States still was required to maintain a relatively large strategic nuclear force capable of holding at risk a wide range of strategic targets and ultimately of inflicting unacceptable damage on an opponent.[9] It was this view of the nature of nuclear deterrence that also led the Clinton administration repeatedly to defend the Anti-Ballistic Missile (ABM) Treaty as the "cornerstone of stability."

The Bush administration argued that the threats of the 21st century were fundamentally different from those the United States had confronted in the past. The 2001 Quadrennial Defense Review contained a stark warning about the threats of the future: Although US military forces enjoy superiority in many dimensions of armed conflict, stated the review, the United States is likely to be challenged by adversaries who possess a wide range of capabilities, including asymmetric approaches to warfare, particularly weapons of mass destruction. The United States cannot predict with a high degree of confidence the identity of the countries or actors that may threaten its interests and security.

9. On the views of the Clinton administration, see Keith Payne, "Post-Cold War Requirements for U.S. Nuclear Deterrence Policy," *Comparative Strategy* (1998), 250–254.

The response to this threat assessment was a proposal by the Bush Administration for a transformation of the US military. Although the main focus of transformation was on conventional forces, the administration's intent was on altering the doctrine and character of the strategic forces.

Two events signalled a doctrinal revolution with respect to American strategic nuclear forces.[10] The first was the decision by the Bush administration on December 14, 2001 to withdraw from the ABM Treaty. The second event was the publication of the Bush administration's Nuclear Posture Review (NPR) on January 9, 2002. The NPR began by acknowledging that the central strategic reality of the Cold War, the East-West conflict, had been replaced by uncertainty. The United States faced the prospect of multiple, potential, opponents with differing or uncertain motives, new sources of conflict, and shifting alliance relationships. As a result, the ability of existing US strategic forces to deter potential aggressors could not be assured. A more flexible doctrine was needed, based on capabilities and approaches that assured friends and allies of the US commitment to their security, dissuaded prospective proliferators from pursuing weapons of mass destruction (WMD), deterred direct threats against the US, its interests, and those of its allies, and promised the defeat of any attack.[11]

The desired force structure to meet these requirements would be built on a spectrum of capabilities rather than focussing on a single threat. The NPR called for "a new strategic triad based on non-nuclear strike forces, strategic defenses, and strategic nuclear forces." The NPR spoke of exploiting synergy between the elements of the new triad.[12]

---

10. Daniel Gouré, n.4.
11. Ibid.
12. Ibid.

The NPR clearly stated a more nuanced role for the strategic nuclear forces than had been the case over the past decade. This new, smaller, strategic nuclear force posture would be structured to address a wide range of immediate and potential contingencies. Adaptive planning would supplement or even replace the Single Integrated Operational Plan (SIOP) with its emphasis "on pre-planned, relatively inflexible, and often massive strike packages."[13]

Generally accepted without much criticism, the seemingly controversial aspects of the NPR were the set of contingencies for nuclear planning and the recommendation that the United States begin the development of new types of nuclear weapons. As reported by the *Los Angeles Times* (March 9, 2002), the classified version of the NPR identified a set of possible contingencies, which includes an Arab-Israeli conflict or a threat from the 'rogue states'. Observers were quick to point out that the NPR's recommendations were a logical extension of the post-September security environment and made sense in terms of the new threats confronting the United States.[14]

Though the NPR made a strong commitment to a large and flexible strategic nuclear capability, it failed to explicitly define the purposes of those strategic nuclear forces. The wide range of contingencies, however, made it more arduous to define an apt force structure and force posture for the remaining strategic nuclear forces. This feature takes on even greater importance in light of the uncertainties regarding when and how the United States might become involved in a nuclear crisis. It speaks only of "immediate, unexpected, and potential" contingencies. Such

13. Ibid.

14. Loren Thompson, "How to Stop Worrying and Love the Bomb," *Wall Street Journal* (March 17, 2002), in Gouré, ibid. Most of the work put in here in based on what Gouré has written and is extensively quoted or referred to. His article is comprehensive and excellent.

contingencies could include "surprise military developments." These formulations are insufficient as the basis for sustained support of nuclear forces and their supporting infrastructure. There is no context on which to draw in order to understand reports that the military has been ordered to develop contingency plans to strike rogue states or to employ small nuclear weapons in limited numbers as so-called "bunker busters".

The National Institute for Public Policy study notes, "a force structure based on a variety of platforms insures against sudden changes in the threat that might make one leg of the triad vulnerable". It also provides for flexibility and responsiveness, critical characteristics in a force that must deal with uncertainty and even surprise.

The size of the American strategic arsenal may be an important contributing factor to both dissuasion and deterrence. Such a force structure, it is believed, particularly deployed in multiple basing modes, "will serve to complicate any would-be attackers' strike planning". In the event of a nuclear conflict, a large arsenal can ensure that no potential adversary would see any advantage from attacking the United States.

Yeltsin and Putin accepted security doctrines that appeared to reject the "no-first-use" restriction that the Soviet Union had once embraced. The one positive aspect which went on to nullify fears of a nuclear conflict was that NATO was basking under the confidence that it no more had an intention of launching aggression against Russia.

The Future Force Posture

The United States has reduced its nuclear arsenal from some 27,000 weapons in the stockpile that existed at the height of the Cold War. By 2012, the number of weapons actually deployed on launchers will be reduced to between 1,700 and 2,200. The collapse of the Warsaw Pact and the Soviet Union, the decline of the Russian military, and the abandonment by the Russian military of the Soviet-era doctrine of seeking to "fight and win a major nuclear war", further shrank the strategic target list.

But the world remains a dangerous place, with a new set of threats, neither well defined nor completely understood. These new forms of threats may not be deterrable by traditional measures. As Robert Walpole noted, "the probability that a missile with a weapon of mass destruction will be used against U.S. forces or interests is higher today than during most of the Cold War."

This seems to suggest that nuclear weapons may actually become more important to American security. The threat of conventional retaliation alone may not be enough. An adversary may seek to acquire weapons of mass destruction in order to counter US conventional superiority. While non-nuclear strike capabilities broaden the range of options available to the US to counter a threat or a conflict, these capabilities cannot take the place of credible strategic nuclear forces.

In such a case, the United States would look for a strategic nuclear force posture that is "large, responsive, flexible, and credible". The United States, then, would need to maintain the existing triad of strategic bombers, ICBMs, and SLBMs. STRATCOM, then, must have the planning capabilities to develop a wide range of weapons employment options, even for a highly selective use of new types of nuclear weapons. The nuclear infrastructure must be sufficient enough to ensure not only the safety and surety of remaining nuclear weapons but also assure the long-term viability of US strategic nuclear forces.[15]

IV

Many of the arguments surrounding deterrence policy during the Cold War, and military interventions till the 1990s

15. Daniel Gouré, n.4.

and even the 'war against terrorism' are fashioned in the language of the theologians, philosophers and jurists who created the Just War tradition to a great measure. Most of the key works establishing and refining the tradition was created in the period of Ambrose, Augustine, Suarez, Vitoria, and Grotius. The last few decades and more have witnessed some very interesting creativity in writing about Just War; and one of the best historians of this tradition is none other than James Turner Johnson, whose works takes us through a reading of Just War from its origins to the modern world.

The main concern now is the problems that have arisen with the Just War tradition especially in the light of attacks such as the 9/11. Will the tradition survive these problems? While the pacifists hold that war is never legitimate and the evolution of the European state system held that in war anything goes; the Just War tradition stands for a certain restraint – *what* we can legitimately fight for and *how* we may legitimately fight. The apostolic letter of the American Catholic Bishops brought to the open some of the important issues of morality which in fact are difficult to deal with when they are confronted. It should be realised that the military and political elites of many countries have interpreted or refer to the Just War tradition and many an international agreement to which the tradition contributed – referred to as laws of war – are seen in principally legal rather than just moral or ethical terms.

In 1983, the US Conference of Catholic Bishops issued the famous Pastoral Letter on nuclear war at the height of the controversy over the nuclear freeze and the deployment of American Pershing and cruise missiles in Europe (to counter the Soviets' installation of intermediate-range SS20s in their part of Europe). Not surprisingly, the bishops found that deterrence, which rested, of course, on an American threat to launch a nuclear attack, violated Just War theory: "It is not morally acceptable", they stated, "to intend to kill the innocent as part of a strategy of deterring nuclear war."[16] Twenty years later, the bishops have again invoked Just War theory to argue for the immorality of a pre-emptive war on Iraq—"We fear that resort to war...would not meet the strict conditions in Catholic teaching for overriding the strong presumption against the use of military force".[17]

Nicholas Rennger has clearly highlighted a very important factor. The laws of war developed during the late 19th and 20th centuries concerned themselves primarily with what it was that was permissible to do in war than with the circumstances under which war should be waged. Emphasis gradually shifted more and more towards fighting a 'bloodless' war in 'humane' ways (as far as the country's own armed forces were concerned). The moot point of concern happens to be that in a war, powers have the tendency to become more, not less, arbitrary. Hence the tendency to move against any feature that was more likely to prompt a war.[18]

Just War stood for a 'just cause', which meant defence of the non-combatants against an armed attack, and punishment of the amoral. In the contemporary context it means national self defence against an armed attack – even retaliation. It makes one wonder if humanitarian intervention was initiated under the cover of the old Just War feature of just cause – the protection of the innocents.

A moral dilema is posed when one questions whether turning a blind eye to the exploits of the flagitious, thus, rendering them ever more daring and insolent is more of a danger, or is it acting unilaterally to counter such pariahs, thus, undermining the legal foundations and leading to a

---

16. Admiral Richard Mies, "The Changing World of Nuclear Deterrence," *Air Force Magazine,* Vol.84, No.9 (September 2001).
17. Charles Krauthammer, n.5.
18. John Mueller, *Retreat from Doomsday: The Obsolescence of Major War* [New York: Basic Books, 1989).

situation of "might is right"? Here is a conflict between legality and ethics and expedience.

The answer is – "what is legal is not always moral and what is legitimate is not invariably legal." Thus, what constitutes "just cause"? Self-defence, as a reaction to direct and overwhelming armed aggressions, is a justified *casus beli.* The use of force is now to be assessed in the light of need to prevent or ameliorate "a permanent humanitarian crisis; pre-empt a clear danger of aggression against what Grotius called 'immediate danger'; peacekeeping operations and enforce compliance with international or bilateral treaties between the aggressor and the attacked state or the attacked state and a third party; honor one's obligations to frameworks and treaties of collective self-defense; secure a safe environment for urgent and indispensable humanitarian relief operations; prevent crimes against humanity or violations of international law by the attacked state; suppress armed infiltration, indirect aggression, or civil strife aided and abetted by the attacked state; protect one's citizens or the citizens of a third party inside the attacked state; respond to an invitation by the authorities of the attacked state – and with their expressed consent – to militarily intervene within the territory of the attacked state; respond to offenses against the nation's honor or its economy".

Whilst the Just War theory calls for a greater degree of responsibility regarding war and during war, the doctrine of nuclear deterrence propagates a sense of safety and peacetime which transcend the Just War theory. John Keegan notes, there was great concern with the justice of the Second World War, amongst politicians, militia and public opinion, but towards the end of the War, aggressive fundamentalism seems to have become part of at least the American view point. The British also displayed wide streaks of aggressive fundamentalism, especially when Winston Churchill epitomised the position by stating that "this atomic bomb is the second coming in wrath". Unfortunately, as Walter Wink points out, "just war theory often seems more intent on finding a way around the binding intentions of its own criteria ... in the name of the bloodiest ideology of our time – nationalism."[19] However, the deterrence theory has led to the development of more complex weapons and it is for this reason that atomic weapons have assisted in rendering the Just War theory useless in regard to proportionality, and violates the precept concerning innocent civilians.

Murray writes that "nuclear weapons will not remain the only agents of mass destruction."[20] Already "several aggressive states have shown interest in developing chemical and biological weapons, which are less expensive and easier to deliver."[21] These weapons violate the proportionality norm of the classical Just War theory. Proportionality and the harming of innocent civilians do not sit easily with the technology of such weapons. Heisbourg comments that it was the Japanese sect of Aum Shinrikyo that funded research into the development of Sarin, used it and are alleged to be carrying out further research. Terrorist activities ironically do not respect the Just War requirement that a war be declared by a rightful authority.[22]

The question of responsibility for the use of these weapons is also one which urgently needs raising. At present, the classical precepts of the Just War theory urge for the promotion of

19. Walter Wink, "Beyond Pacifism and Just War", *Life and Peace Review*, Vol.6, No.2 (1992), p.5.
20. Williamson A Murray, "The Age of Mechanised Warfare", in Geoffrey Parker (ed.), *Cambridge History of Warfare* (Oxford: Cambridge University Press, 1995), p. 371.
21. Ibid.
22. Francois Heisbourg, *The Future of Modern Warfare* (London: Phoenix, 1997).

responsibility and fairness during wartime, but the violation of all these principles seems to be possible by the use of 'just weapon'.

With the speedy progress in nuclear weapons development and sophistication in tactics, Just War theorists have continued to be perturbed by the chances of their use during times of conflict.[23] James Turner Johnson notes Ramsey's approach and comments thus: "Ramsey argued that the Christian Just War theory is based on the moral duty of love of neighbour. The obligation to protect the neighbour who is being attacked provides justification for Christians to resort to force; at the same time, love also imposes limits on such force requiring that no more be done to the unjust assailant than is necessary to prevent the evil he would do, and that no justified use of force ever can itself directly and intentionally target the innocent."[24] This perspective believes in rationality of the enemy. This response is excellent in concept, in reality it has very little meaning when applied directly to a situation.

The Just War theory appears to have very little application to the field of warfare in an age where science is used by some to invent weapons that are lethal – more than the normal expected level. "The just war theory cannot cope with cybernetic technology."

Hence, strategies fashioned to diminish the harm of nuclear warfare, to ensure a greater control over targeting policies in a nuclear war, are regarded as lacking in adequate prevention of the risk of probable increases in nuclear exchange. When national interest, as perceived by a nation, is at stake, morality

---

23. Paul Ramsey, *The Just War - Force and Political Responsibility* (USA: University Press of America, 1983).
24. J T Johnson, *Can Modern War Be Just?* (New Haven, CT:Yale University Press 1984). Also, Y Turan Çetiner "Is Nuclear Deterrence Morally Acceptable?", *Perceptions:Journal of International Affairs*, Vol.III, No.1 (March-May 1998), pp.104-116.

is the last thing on their minds. [25] A response is justified on the grounds that the action taken was what they considered to be the correct option. Morality in the garb of self restraint is in use only as long as an attack is not under way.

Former Assistant Secretary of Defence, Joseph S Nye, pointed out that to consider the morality of means without considering the morality of ends is a narrow approach. He stated the five maxims of nuclear ethics to be: i) self defence – a just but limited cause, ii) never treating nuclear weapons as normal weapons, iii) minimising the harm to innocent people, iv) reducing the risk of nuclear war in the near term and, lastly, v) reducing reliance on nuclear weapons over a period of time.[26]

According to Herman Kahn, nuclear weapons are neither moral nor immoral, but they can be used to accomplish moral objectives in morally acceptable ways. Kahn went on to oppose the use of nuclear weapons against non-nuclear enemies on the grounds of the principle of proportionality.[27]

The other side of the argument that upholds morality of use of nuclear weapons is that use of nuclear weapons in retaliations or their use *against* an aggression is morally less objectionable than their use *for* aggression. Robert McNamara estimated that a US retaliation would have to be capable of destroying one-quarter to one-third of the Soviet population, and one-half to two-thirds of its industrial capacity.[28]

A totalitarian country may judge others by its perception of morality and justify its use of nuclear weapons by its own

---

25. Y Turan Çetiner, n. 24.
26. Ibid
27. Ibid
28. Stephen J. Cimbala, "Strategic War Termination: The Missing Element", in Stephen J. Cimbala and Joseph D. Douglas Jr. (eds.) (1988), *Ending a Nuclear War: Are the Superpowers Prepared?*, Exeter, p. 158.

understanding and sense of ethics. As of now, even the pre-emption option is regarded as serving a higher form of deterrence.

V

The timultuous shift from Cold War to groping for an enemy, to the challenges of facing the unconventional is unimaginable.[29] Morality of "deterrence" is replaced by the objective of strengthening ways to wage a "preventive war." The "humanitarian [military] intervention" in Somalia, Bosnia, Rwanda and Liberia are the new faces of conflict control mechanisms. These conflicts and the dawn of wars waged by terrorists have mutilated the theory of Just War – it is a reversal of fight in the name of God for what they believe are 'just cause(s)'.

The Bishops had disputed the morality of nuclear deterrence, proposing conditional support for a policy that promoted progress in reduction of nuclear stockpile. For Michael Novak, the essential ingredients that ended the Cold War are still valid. The "work of peace is basically the work of politics."[30]

Deterrence did work in the past, when there were only two actors. And even "under those circumstances, deterrence was psychologically debilitating, inherently unstable, and highly dangerous." And to choose it as "the principle on which to rest our safety in this age of weapons of mass destruction", of one's own accord, is sheer folly.[31]

What then is the role of strategic nuclear forces in providing a strategy that would be to the best of U.S. strategic advantage?

---

29. "Twenty years after peace pastoral, a call for new approaches", *World National Catholic Reporter,* November 21, 2003 by Joe Feuerherd, in the *National Catholic Reporter* (Washington, 2003), http://www.findarticles.com/p/articles/mi_m1141/is_5_40/ai_110808661.

30. Ibid.

31. Charles Krauthammer is a contributing editor to The Weekly Standard. http://www.theweeklystandard.com/Content/Public/Articles/000/000/001/964dzkuf.asp?pg=2

The idea of the US administration is, in fact, to maintain a strategic nuclear force of "sufficing size, flexibility, and responsiveness" so that any opponent will be deterred from attempting to use such weapons as a means of offense. The most probable and essential strategic problem that could confront the United States is the deterrence or defeat of local aggression, including the possible use of WMD. It is not clear whether the threat of a proportional response would be sufficient to deter some adversaries. The idea is to have credible limited nuclear strike options that can reasonably be expected to deter the use of WMD by an opponent facing conventional defeat.[32] It also requires the development of intelligence capabilities that could help in case of retaliation in the event of covert use of WMD by a state. This is basically a tactic of dissuasion. It is noteworthy in this context that the United States announced dropping its 1978 pledge not to use nuclear weapons against non-nuclear states. Another role is to hold as hostage those targets that are highly prized by a potential adversary but that are not accessible by conventional means.

Also, the aim of the US would be to undertake measures to prevent Russia and China from using their strategic forces as a 'means of escalation control'.

This is a period in the history of security when many nations are moving towards self reliance in defence and are tempted to pursue their own WMD capabilities as a means of deterring regional threats.

In the present international environment, it is difficult to design a force-sizing adequate for the expansive range of

32. Molly Clark, Herbert Scoville Jr Peace Fellow, "The Bush Doctrine: Pre-emption And Dominance : The National Security Strategy of the United States of America", Fact Sheet October 2002 (This is a publication of Physicians for Social Responsibility's Center for Global Security and Health). http://www.psr.org

situations in which nuclear weapons might be relevant. On the basis of such a perception, on September 20, 2002, the Bush administration published the 38-page document titled, "The National Security Strategy of the United States of America". It lays emphasis on unilateralism and international military dominance by the US. It rejects the strategy of deterrence and in its place the emphasis is on pre-emptive strikes to deal with the proliferation of weapons of mass destruction (WMD) – a fact unprecedented in American history. The idea is to seek out and destroy suspected stores of enemy WMD before they can be used against the US The focus is more on *striking first to prevent the mere possibility of such an attack occurring over the long-term* (emphasis added).[33]

The Bush administration has indicated its plans for the development of a "bunker-buster," a tactical nuclear weapon with a low enough explosive yield to be deemed usable for preemptive missions aimed at destroying underground stores of WMD.[34] In the event that a WMD site is mistargeted and innocent civilians get killed, the international community will lose whatever little reason they have, to trust the US estimates of suspected WMD sites even if they are accurate.

The Administration had requested $15.5 million for the development of such a weapon in the FY2003 Defence

---

33. President George W Bush, The National Security Strategy of the United States of America, September 2002, http://www.whitehouse.gov/nsc/print/nssall.html

34. "The Bush National Security Strategy: A First Step," Center for Defense Information, http://www.cdi.org/national-security-strategy/washington. cfm. Also read "Uncovered Nukes: A Fact Sheet on Tactical Nuclear Weapons," Council for a Livable World: Coalition to Reduce Nuclear Dangers, http://www.clw.org/pub/clw/coalition/briefv5n19.htm; and "Background on the Robust Nuclear Earth Penetrator," Friends Committee on National Legislation, http://www.fcnl.org/issues/arm/aup/min_earth-pentratr5102.htm

Authorization Bill.[35] Any nuclear use by the United States in a pre-emptive strike carries with it the threat of nuclear, biological, or chemical retaliation against United States by either the targeted state or perhaps even its allies.

This policy and its implementation at some stage are good precedents for other states to follow suit and unilaterally and pre-emptively target its enemies. Ironically, the United States could itself be the target. Russia cited this document to justify pre-emptive strikes against Chechen rebels in Georgia.[36] The Chinese reaction is to focus on the new strategy's implications for pre-emptive attacks on North Korea (identified as a major WMD producer in the document), and on the document's restatement of "US commitments to the self-defense of Taiwan." This document will, thus, pose diplomatic and other problems too.

The US is not exactly unaware, what with its experience of the September 2001 attacks that awesome military might or firepower do not necessarily guarantee victory against a determined (fanatic) nation or group of people out to attain their objective at shocking and, most of the time, unreasonable cost. Objectives tend to blind rationality. Objectives and means to attain them have to be searched without falling back on the trusted and available strategies. Increasing one's strength without altering how others perceive your intentions, make the environment more insecure, wrote Lieutenant Colonel J D Perry and Dr Steven Metz. What's more, the architects of deterrence need to understand the dynamics of perception and communication.[37]

35. Council on Foreign Relations, "The Iraq Debate: National Security Strategy," http://www.cfr.org/background/background_iraq_nationalsecurity.php, 1.
36. Refer to Bennett Roth, "Bush Outlines Strike Policy," *The Monterey County Herald*, September 21, 2002, 2.
37. Lieutenant Colonel J D Parry and Dr Steven Metz, in *Military Review* (5/1989) in their article on "The Principles of Deterrence", *Universal MIlitary Abstracts*, pp.10 & 11.

6

Conclusion

I

The Cold War has been the defining phenomenon for the past five decades. Though the super powers were deterred, there were conflicts between the allies of the two as well as contests for political power in Europe, Asia and the Third World. Fear and challenge had dominated arms control and detente. There were crises over rights in Berlin, war in Korea, ballistic missile crisis in Cuba, and protracted and agonising war in Vietnam. However, though the case may not be always so, open nuclear threats have been ineffective and their frequency often exaggerated. There have been, fortunately, differences between doctrine and behaviour, theory and practice. Today, the race for nuclear weapon superiority is far less pronounced than it was since the time the first two bombs were dropped in August 1945. Throughout the period of Cold War, the United States and the Soviet Union had plenty of survivable nuclear overkill capacity. The Russians, including the Soviet leadership, remembered the immense casualties they suffered during a "merely conventional" Second World War. This had no match in the entire history of the United States. The peril induced by nuclear deterrence was not affected by the relative ruthlessness or sufferings of the American and Soviet societies. The imperative of avoiding a nuclear war imposed caution on the leaders so much so that it led Raymond Aron to conclude that there was "a solidarity of Great Powers against a total war of which they would be the first victims." They remained determined not to destroy themselves. Despite detailed war-plans and frantic efforts to evolve strategies for fighting and prevailing in a nuclear war, leaders of both sides remained sane and they were also watched and adviced by sane colleagues.[1]

At the moment of choice, the nuclear threat was put into practice.[2] There were nuclear alerts but they were part of coercive diplomacy. The "tradition of non-use of nuclear weapons", as Thomas Schelling called it, "is the most important legacy of the first half century of fission." While NATO military doctrine never renounced first use of nuclear weapons in an armed conflict with the Warsaw Pact, a circumstance never arose to implement NATO strategy in Europe. Thus, the most dangerous moments in Cold War history have also been the most revealing ones regarding non-use. The confrontation with US on Cuba and on a lesser scale with China over a long common border was resolved peacefully. Soviet caution further enhanced this tradition. Such a sharing of the same tradition has, however, set a strong foundation for arms control moves and declarations of non-use of weapons all these years. Both, history and logic, have made it clear that nuclear weapons will never be used unless it is in the hands of the most irrational or the insane. "There is no level of superiority", states Bundy, "which will make a strategic first strike between the two great states anything but an act of utter folly."[3] It was in such a scenario, when nothing would be better and welcome

1. McGeorge Bundy, *Danger and or Survival: Choices About the Bombing in the First Fifty Years* (New York: Random House, 1988), p.587.
2. Ibid.
3. Ibid, p.589.

than arms reductions, that President Gorbachev and President Regan moved in the same direction and they declared in 1987, "A nuclear war cannot be won and must never be fought."

After several years of discussion and Reagan Administration's plans to fight and win a protracted nuclear war, this new trend was a remarkable admission of shared danger. The coming into power of Mikhail Gorbachev in the Soviet Union in 1985, is a watershed in the history of nuclear confrontation between the two super powers. His policies of Perestroika and Glasnost opened a Pandora's Box in his country and within the Warsaw Pact. Global tensions were lowered thereby creating an environment favourable to serious disarmament negotiations. The INF Treaty of 1987, eliminating a whole category of nuclear weapons from Europe resulted from major concessions made by the Soviet Union. Gorbachev's policies eventually culminated in the reunification of Germany, the dissolution of the Warsaw Pact and finally the disintegration of the Soviet Union itself (1989-1991).

According to Zbigniew Brzezinski, the disintegration of the Soviet Union is an outcome no less decisive and one sided than the defeat of Napoleon's France in 1875 or of imperial Germany in 1918 or of Nazi Germany and imperial Japan in 1945. It is an event of great historical magnitude which had a direct impact on nuclear deterrent strategy of the US. The gigantic structure of nuclear deterrence was evolved as a deterrent to the Soviet threats. With the disappearance of the threat, nuclear war plans lost their relevance.[4]

One major change of great symbolic significance in the context of nuclear war fighting strategy occurred as the Cold

4. Z Brzezinski, "The Cold War and its Aftermath", *Foreign Affairs* (Fall 1992), p. 34.

War was ending. The United States' Strategic Air Command Post – the so-called Doomsday plane – which had been in the air since July 3, 1961, was grounded at the Air Force base in Omaha on July 24, 1990.[5] There is no such situation as yet in the contemporary period where the US may have to make the painful choice between defeat and first-use of nuclear weapons or fear each other's intentions (viz. Russia). This is one important outcome and meaning of the 1989-91 transformation of Europe.

McGeorge Bundy, who was special assistant on national security to President Kennedy, and was intimately involved in the decision-making during the Cuban Missile Crisis of October 1962, has made an observation which puts nuclear targeting in a realistic perspective. He says that a single strategic nuclear warhead on a single military target would be the worst ever since the Second World War. A hundred warheads on targets would be an instantaneous and terrible disaster; and a thousand warheads would be a catastrophe beyond all human experience. This observation should be compared with the SIOP targeting schemes to realise how unrealistic and genocidal they were.[6]

After the dissolution of the Warsaw Pact and the disintegration of the Soviet Union, the US had two distinctions:-

- It was the least threatened of major states.
- It is the one state with modern unmatched conventional weapons.

Nuclear weapons cannot be abolished as the know-how remains but the great powers showed their keenness to

5. M Zuberi, "Security Concerns After the Cold War", paper presented at the United Nation's Regional Disarmament Workshop for Asia and the Pacific, Bandung, (Indonesia), January 1991, in *Disarmament* (New York : UN Department of Disarmament Affairs, 1991).
6. Bundy, n.1.

subdue the importance of these weapons as a means of security. Between them the two sides had some fifty thousand nuclear warheads. This was the most massive single threat to humanity. This is about 95% of the world's total stock. These were, thus, enormous arsenals to maintain a non-use policy. And, the threat posed by these enormous arsenals was a cause of concern for the leaders of the two super powers. Before the disintegration of the Soviet Union, President Bush and Gorbachev signed the START-I in 1991. It was a comprehensive treaty of unprecedented scope with verification arrangements, which were more remarkable than the reductions themselves were. START I was the product of nine years of negotiations, 250 pages of annexes, texts and protocols buttressed by another 30 pages of related agreements, letters, correspondence, joint and other statements and declarations. The treaty governed each side's intercontinental ballistic missiles, SLBMs and heavy bombers. For over forty years these weapons were the mainstay of the US approach to security through deterrence. Because of the continued reliance on these weapons throughout the Cold War period, the negotiations were prolonged – for over two decades – and difficult. Each side ascertaining whether the other side had an advantage. The result is 800 pages of text.[7]

It broke tradition with the past as it involved actual and significant reductions in the strategic forces of each side. By including direct and equal limits on ballistic missile throw-weight (lift-capability of missiles) and on ballistic missile warheads, the treaty ensured equal rights between the two

7. For nine years the talks which were begun on June 29,1982, were supplemented by several meetings at Geneva, Washington, Houston, Moscow and summit meetings in Geneva 1985, Reykjavik in 1986, Washington in 1987, Moscow in 1988, Malta in 1989 and Washington in 1990. On July 31, 1991, the Treaty was signed at the Moscow summit.

sides. Verification was the most extensive and intrusive ever negotiated – it promoted openness and military transparency to an extent not feasible in the past. Verification was possible through the following measures:-

- Data and notification exchange.
- National Technical Means (NTM) of verification in combination with "co-operative measures", display in the open, at the request of another party of the triad to enhance the efficiency of the NTMs.
- Access to telemetric information.
- Exhibition and inspections of twelve different kinds.
- Monitoring of the ICBM production facilities for more launchers of ICBMSs with a view to confirming the number of missiles produced for mobile launchers.
- Establishment of the Joint Compliance and Inspections Commission to resolve the issues related to compliance with the obligations.
- To resolve issues related to the extension of the corresponding provisions to new kinds of weapons.[8]

The Treaty was designed to be relevant for more than its fifteen years duration, if the parties agreed to its extension. Each side was limited to:-

- 1600 strategic nuclear delivery vehicles, which is 36% below the Soviet level and 29% below the US level (of that time).
- 6000 total accountable warheads (41%-43%).
- 4900 accountable warheads deployed in ICBMs or SLBMs (48%- 50%).

8. Yuri Nazarkin, "Strategic Nuclear Disarmament in a New Era", *Disarmament*, Vol. 14, No.2 (1992), pp.27-28. The author was the head of the Soviet delegation to START Talks.

- 1540 accountable warheads deployed on 154 heavy ICBMs (US has no heavy ICBMs, 50% of Soviet).
- 1100 accountable warheads deployed on mobile ICBMs.[9]
- An aggregate throw weight of deployed ICBMs & SLBMs equalling 3600 million metric tonnes (US throw weight falls below this level and, thus, no decrease was required; 54% of Soviet).

The deepest reductions that were sought were in the Soviet SS-18 heavy ICBMs to move towards less threatening and more survivable systems, such as heavy bombers. Thus, there was to be a reduction – 1/3 of strategic warheads to a total on each side of 6100 to 8600.

In the eighteen months after START I, the United States and Russia reached a "Joint Understanding" in June 1992 which led to START II in January 1993. It prescribed further reductions in strategic weapons. Reinforcing the Bush-Gorbachev proposals was the support of the American initiative by the Joint Chiefs of Staff and the apparent parallel approval of Russian military leaders. For the Americans, the Gulf War was a relevant experience: the armed forces had learnt what their best conventional forces can do and it was more than enough. With the absence of mistrust as existed in the Cold War period, the requirement of tactical nuclear weapons was less.

Only one basic requirement remained for the strategic forces of the two powers: they were to be "considered fully adequate...to ensure against strategic attack from the other."[10]

---

9. Ibid, p 22. As of Septembers I, 1990, the aggregate throw-weight of deployed ballistic missiles was 6,623.3 tons for the USSR and 2,361.3 tons for the US.

10. McGeorge Bundy, William Crowe, Sydney D Drell, *Reducing Nuclear Danger: The Road Away From the Brink* (New York: Council of Foreign Relations Press, 1993), p.31.

This deterrent requirement has been central to both sides throughout the nuclear age, and today it is the only requirement. It is interesting, however, to note that Bundy, Crowe and Drell advice the need to continue maintaining a superpower balance even though at a lesser level. They state thus: "Fifty years of experience argue strongly against any confidence in extreme solutions. In particular there is no early escape through either the achievement of strategic superiority or the abolition of nuclear weapons."[11]

The survivability, safety and absence of hair trigger danger go up as the number of warheads comes down. These are well protected aspects of START I and II, all with the broad support of both countries. The START-II negotiations especially dealt with these aspects. The number of warheads for the US and Russia (including those located in Belarus; Kazakhstan and Ukraine) had been fixed at 3,500 to 3000 respectively.

It must, however, be pointed out that even the reductions promised for in START-I and II was not going to deprive the United States and Russia of an overkill nuclear capacity by the beginning of the 21st century. Secretary of State, Warren Christopher, had assured the US Senate that the American stockpile after START-II would still "have a capacity to destroy civilization as we know it several times over."[12]

This seems to strengthen the opinion of Bundy, Crowe and Drell when they wrote, "The United States should respect the reality that as long as there are bombs there will be a nuclear danger that is unique in all history. The bomb is uniquely dangerous because it is uniquely destructive – so destructive ... that no one chose to use it or to provoke its

11. Ibid, p.32.
12. Quoted in M Zuberi, "Nuclear Arms Control", *World Focus* (May 1993), p.3.

use by others. That reality must permeate American policy choices more thoroughly in the future than in the past."[13]

II

There have been three broad groups of experts engaged in the debate on nuclear strategy:-

- The deterers and arms controllers.
- The targeteers.
- The disarmers.

The first group consisted of Deterers and Arms Controllers. They attempted to ensure the benefits of nuclear deterrence while reducing and minimising its dangers through arms controls. Their endeavour was to manage the security dilemmas of the nuclear age. Advocates of stable nuclear deterrence believed that a prudent management of the international system was possible. This group included the mainstream American writers on nuclear strategy including Bernard Brodie, Thomas Schelling, Henry Kissinger, Herman Kahn, Morton Halperin and others.

The second group may be called the Targeteers, who were committed to the belief that the best way to prevent a nuclear war was to prepare to fight and win it. Nuclear weapons may be destructive but the basic logic of warfare remained unchanged. They believed that these weapons had not only political but also military utility; that the prime target of nuclear weapons should be the adversary's military capability even if this involved the slaughter of civilians on a massive scale as a 'collateral' damage; that usable and controlable limited nuclear options were both necessary and possibly that nuclear deterrence can best be achieved

---

13. Bundy, Crowe, Drell, n.10, p.141.

through a demonstrable capacity for nuclear war-fighting. This group included James Schlesinger, Albert Wohlstetter, Colin Gray and members of the post Reagan administration. Not surprisingly, this group regarded the Disarmers as hopelessly naïve and deterers and arms controllers as simply misguided.

Believing that nuclear deterrence itself has been the main engine of the arms race at the nuclear and conventional levels, the disarmers have emphasised the ethical dilemmas of deterrence. There are various constituents of thinking represented in this group. Some were concerned about the possibilities of accidental or inadvertent nuclear war because of the hair-trigger levels of command and control systems. Their objections to nuclear deterrence were based on prudential calculations. Others including those who derived some of the assumptions from the Just War traditions objected to nuclear deterrence on moral points. George Kennan, Michael Walzer, Paul Ramsey, James Turner Johnson represent these two strands. The Pastoral Letter of the American Catholic Bishops attempted to continue the two strands of thought thereby becoming a powerful critique of the American nuclear strategy.

Robert McNamara briefly flirted with counter-force targeting and then settled on deterrence through Assured Destruction. It seemed simple, logical and especially attractive, and, for McNamara, quantifiable. But war fighters tore Assured Destruction to pieces by pointing out that it was immoral and a genocidal strategy.

The weakness of the doctrine of nuclear deterrence has been – what would happen if deterrence should fail. The strategist's answer was – be prepared to fight a nuclear war at all levels up to Assured Destruction in the hope that war would be kept at lowest level. Nuclear war fighting, in their view, was critical to nuclear deterrence. In the name of being able to fight a nuclear war, should deterrence fail, the United Sates developed new generations of nuclear weapons. They proposed Assured Survival through SDI. But even this was no guarantee for survival.

Despite an overlapping in the position of the Deterers, Arms Controllers and the Targeteers, they were invited to discourse on the nature of the problem of nuclear weapons and its appropriate solutions. Much of the debate can be seen in terms of integration among these broad groups and the positions they advocated.

The nuclear debate remained inconclusive because of the rather sudden end of the Cold War and the unforeseen disintegration of a nuclear super power. The nuclear danger has certainly been reduced but belief in the beneficial effect of nuclear weapons is still firmly shared.

III

It has never been really easy to come up with a clearly defined policy that would contain nothing regrettable or destructive. This is clearly evident in the various attempts to formulate a moral perspective on deterrence policy. Given the enormity of the destruction that is bound to occur in a nuclear war, moral reasoning must pay primary attention to consequences. There are unavoidable uncertainties in the estimation of risks because sound ethical judgments will be contingent on empirical facts and hypothetical arguments about strategic interactions and values.

On the other hand, the pacifists rightly conclude that the possession and threat of use of nuclear weapons are immoral and those who justify the limited use of nuclear weapons do so generally as part of the larger argument about deterrence. For example, the use.of tactical intermediate range nuclear weapons in defence of Europe was justified as the best way to deter a Soviet conventional and nuclear aggression against NATO.[14] Those

14. Pierce S Corden, "Ethics and Deterrence: Moving Beyond the Just War Tradition", in Harold Ford and Francis X. Winters (eds), *Ethics and Nuclear Strategy* (New York: Maryknoll, Orbis, 1977), p.168.

whose strategies include such views must face the paradoxes and the ambiguities inherent in the doctrine of nuclear deterrence. These ambiguities arise from the very logic of the theory. The very idea that there exist missiles, thousands of miles away, capable of massive destruction within a few minutes of launching is highly immoral and incomprehensible.[15]

Archbishop Hunthausen pointed out the dangers of continued dependence on nuclear weapons. He also drew attention to the risks involved in any move for unilateral disarmament. What is required is a proper blend of moral and political reasoning to enhance national security. If deterrence has to work even as a provisional measure it has "to be ascertained what the morally right course is, not what the morally wrong course is."[16] Germain Grisez adviced the unilateral renunciation of the policy of deterrence, fully aware that deterrence is futile without the threat to civilians.[17]

For Richard Falk, "nuclear weaponry is totally unacceptable as an element of security policy. It is unacceptable for the same reason that torture and terrorism are unacceptable, and no tactical, pragmatic argument as to effectiveness can overcome such fundamental objections."[18] His conclusion merits note. "We have lived now for several generations

---

15. Edward N Luttwak, "How to Think About Nuclear War", *Commentary* 14 (August 1982), pp.21-28.
16. Archbishop Raymond Hunthausen's address to the Pacific North West Synod of Lutheran Church in America. July 12, 1981, mentioned in R. Hehir (ed) *Nuclear Disarmament: Key Statements of Pope, Bishops, Councils and Churches* (New York: Paulist Press, 1968), p.34.
17. G Grisez, "Towards a Consistent Natural Law Ethics of Killing", *American Journal of Jurisprudence* 15 (1970), p.93 in David Hollenbach, *Nuclear Ethics: A Christian Moral Argument* (New York: Paulist Press, 1983), p.70.
18. R Falk, "New Realities: Disarmament, Peace Building and Global Security", *Disarmament* (1993), p.90.

relying on weaponry that would have been criminalized at the end of World War II had the atom bomb been developed by Germany and used against British cities rather than developed by the winning side in what was widely perceived as a just war."[19]

By June 1, 1994, the United States had de-targeted all of its strategic nuclear missiles pointed at locations in former Soviet Union for the first time in 35 years. This was in keeping with the pledge of the Moscow Declaration signed by Yeltsin and Clinton on January 14, 1994, whereby they agreed not to target their nuclear missiles against each other or against any other country. *The missiles will instead be targeted towards the seas.* Russia had also de-targeted its strategic nuclear missiles. The implementation of this decision was completed by May 30. "Detargeting is an important symbolic point", said Kathleen DeLaski, because it emphasises "the strengthening partnership between the United States and Russia". The implementation of this agreement proved that the two nations are no longer nuclear adversaries.[20] 500 older US Minuteman III were later aimed at the oceans, while the then contemporary Trident and Peacekeeper missiles contained no targeting information at all. Russia went on to join the Partnership for Peace Agreement with NATO. The British also unilaterally detargeted their strategic missiles. Detargeting cannot be verified but retargeting can be verified 'fairly quickly', if need arose.

Philip Noel Baker, a Nobel Prize recipient stated, "The great intelligence of human beings created the evil of atomic weapons. The attitude of many of our politicians who claim that the fear of nuclear and hydrogen weapons prevent conventional wars is a mistake, nothing but a

---

19. Ibid, p.88.
20. "U.S. Detargets All Strategic Nuclear Missiles", news briefing by spokesman DeLaski. Defense Department Report in Backgrounder, *Wireless File*, New Delhi, U.S.I.S, June 1, 1994.

meaningless myth ... humans have the responsibility to do with what they have created."[21]

The year 1995 marked the 50th anniversary of the atomic bombings of Hiroshima and Nagasaki, and the close of World War II. But the warning of Albert Einstein fell on deaf ears. "The release of the atomic energy", stated he, "has so influenced everything that our former ways of thinking have been rendered obsolete. We therefore face catastrophe unheard of in our times. If mankind is to survive, then we need a completely new way of thinking."[22]

For 45 years, from World War I period till the end of Cold War, it was agreed that the greatest threat to global security was an all out war between the two super powers culminating in the use of nuclear weapons.[23] The present era is by no means free of the threat of armed conflicts as demonstrated by the persistent turbulence in international politics, in as diverse areas as Indonesia, Burma, Sri Lanka, Peru, Liberia, Somalia, Yugoslavia and the threats of terrorist strikes, the worst of its illustrations being the 9/11 attacks on America. In this context, the utterances of Henry Kissinger sound true: "A threat meant as a bluff but taken seriously is more useful for purposes of deterrence when a 'genuine' threat is interpreted as a bluff."[24] The atom bomb robbed the survivors of Hiroshima and later Nagasaki of their "bodies, spirits and souls",

21. Hiraoka Takashi, Mayor of Hiroshima, quoted in Falk, n.18, p.8.
22. Ibid, p.9.
23. Michael T Clare, "The New Challenge to Global Security", *Current History* (April 1993), pp.155-161, at p.155.
24. Henry Kissinger (ed), *Problems of National Strategy: A Book of Readings* (New York: Praeger, 1965), p.6.

depriving them of even the normal privilege of living "like human beings".[25] Walzer is no farther from the truth and sentiments of the many who oppose the use of nuclear weapons:

"Nuclear weapons explode the theory of Just War. They are the first of mankind's technological inventions that are simply not compatible within the immediate moral world."[26]

---

25. Takashi, n.21, p.8.
26. M Walzer, *Just and Unjust Wars: A Moral Argument With Historical Illustrations* (New York: Basic Books, 1977), p.282.

Appendix 1

EXCERPTS

Many of the Church statements contain the following elements:-

1) An analysis of relevant Biblical material, including the meaning of the word peace, ethical texts in the Old and the New Testament, etc.
2) An outline of Christian attitudes towards peace and war through the history of the church, including the essential points of the Doctrine of the Just War.
3) An analysis of the present armament situation with special emphasis on deterrence.
4) Recommendations for politicians and governments, Christians and Churches.

The Challenge of Peace: God's Promise and Our Respone: Pastoral Letter on War and Peace by the National Conference of Catholic Bishops of the United States[1] (1983)

Peace in the Modern World : Religious Perspectives and Principles

The nuclear threat transcends religious, cultural and national boundaries. To confront its danger requires all the resources reason and faith can muster.

---

1 *Bulletin of Peace Proposals,* Vol. 15, No. 3 (1984), pp. 244-251.

We do not intend that our treatment of each of these issues carry the same moral authority as our statement of universal moral principles and formal church teaching.

The nature of peace

The Catholic tradition has always understood the meaning of peace in positive terms. Peace is both a gift of God and a human work. It must be constructed on the basis of central human values : truth; freedom and love....

However, the protection of human rights and the preservation of peace are tasks to be accomplished in a world marked by sin and conflict of various kinds.

The Just-War criteria

The moral theory of the 'just war' of 'limited war' doctrine begins with the presumption which binds all Christians : we should do no harm to our neighbours; how we treat our enemy is the key test of whether we love our neighbour; and the possibility of taking even one human life is a prospect we should consider in fear and trembling.

The use of nuclear weapons

For the tradition which acknowledges some legitimate use of force, some important elements of contemporary nuclear strategies move beyond the limits of moral justification. A justifiable use of force must be both discriminatory and proportionate. Certain aspects of both US and Soviet strategies fail both tests. ...On the more complicated issue of 'limited nuclear war', it seems to us that public officials would be unable to refute the following conclusion of the study made by the Pontifical Academy of Sciences :

'Even a nuclear attack directed only at military facilities would be devastating to the country as a whole. This is because military facilities are widespread rather than concentrated at only a few points. Thus, many nuclear weapons would be exploded'.

'Furthermore, the spread of radiation due to the natural winds and atmospheric mixing would kill vast numbers of people and contaminate large areas. The medical facilities of any nation would be inadequate to care for the survivors. An objective examination of the medical situation that would follow a nuclear war leads to but one conclusion : Prevention is our only recourse'.

Moral principles and policy choices

In light of these perspectives we address three questions more explicitly :

1. counterpopulation warfare;
2. initiation of nuclear war; and
3. limited nuclear war.

1. Counterpopulation warfare

Under no circumstances may nuclear weapons or other instruments of mass slaughter be used for the purpose of destroying population centers or other predominantly civilian targets.

Retaliatory action, whether nuclear or conventional, which would indiscriminately take many wholly innocent lives, must also be condemned. This condemnation, in our judgment, applied even to the retaliatory use of weapons striking enemy cities after our own have already been struck.

2. The initiation of nuclear war

We do not perceive any situation in which the deliberate initiation of nuclear warfare on however restricted a scale can be morally justified. Non-nuclear attacks by another state must be resisted by other than nuclear means.

Whether under conditions of war in Europe, parts of Asia, of the Middle East, or the exchange of strategic weapons directly between the United States and the Soviet Union, the difficulties of limiting the use of nuclear weapons are immense. No one can be certain that this escalation would not occur even in the face of political efforts to keep such an exchange 'limited'. We find the moral responsibility of beginning nuclear war not justified by rational political objectives.

We express repeatedly in this letter our extreme scepticism about the prospects for controlling a nuclear exchange, however limited the first use might be. Consequently we seek to reinforce the barrier against any use of nuclear weapons. Our support of a 'no first use' policy must be seen in this light.

At the same time we recognise the responsibility the United States has had, continues to have, in assisting allied nations in their defence against either a conventional or a nuclear attack may require nuclear weapons for a time, even though their possession and development must be subject to rigid restrictions... development of an alternative defence position will still take time.

In light of the probable effects of initiating nuclear war , we urge NATO to move rapidly towards the adoption of a 'no first use' policy, but doing so in tandem with development of an adequate alternative defence posture.

3. Limited nuclear war

It would be possible to agree with our first two conclusions and still not be sure about retaliatory use of nuclear weapons in what is called a 'limited exchange'. The issue at stake is nuclear exchange. We wish to raise a series of questions which challenged the actual meaning of 'limited' in this discussion—

- Would they be able under the conditions of stress, time pressures and fragmentary information to make the extraordinarily precise decision needed to keep the exchange limited if this were technically possible?

- Would military commanders be able in the midst of the destruction and confusion of a nuclear exchange to maintain a policy of 'discriminate targeting'?
- Given the accidents we know about in peacetime conditions, what assurances are there that computer errors could be avoided in the midst of a nuclear exchange? Would not the casualties, even in a war defined as limited by strategists, still run in the millions?
- Unless these questions can be answered satisfactorily, we will continue to be highly sceptical about the real meaning of 'limited'. One of the criteria of the just-war tradition is a reasonable hope of success in brining about justice and peace. We must ask whether such a reasonable hope can exist once nuclear weapons have been exchanged. The burden of proof remains on those who assert that meaningful limitation is possible.
- A nuclear response to either conventional or nuclear attack can cause destruction which goes far beyond 'legitimate defense'. Such use of nuclear weapons would not be justified. We, therefore, express our view that the first imperative is to prevent any use of nuclear weapons and our hope that leaders will resist the notion that nuclear conflict can be limited, contained or won in any traditional sense.

D. Deterrence in principle and practice...

2. The moral assessment of deterrence

...For some, the fact that nuclear weapons have not been used since 1945 means that deterrence has worked, and this fact satisfies the demands of both the political and the moral order.

Targeting doctrine raises significant moral questions becuase it is a significant determinant of what would occur if nuclear weapons were ever to be used. Although we acknowledge the need for deterrent, not all forms of deterrence are morally acceptable. There are moral limits to deterrence policy as well as to policy regarding use. Specifically, it is not morally acceptable to intend to kill the innocent as part of a strategy of deterring nuclear war. The question of whether US policy involves an intention to strike civilian centers (directly targeting civilian populations) has been one of our factual concerns ...

We wish now to make some specific evaluations :

1. If nuclear deterrence exists only to prevent the use of nuclear weapons by others, then proposals to go beyond this to planning for prolonged periods of repeated nuclear strikes and counterstrikes, or 'prevailing' in nuclear war, are not acceptable. This encourages notions that nuclear war can be engaged in with tolerable human and moral consequences. Rather, we must continually say no to the ideas of nuclear war.
2. If nuclear deterrence is our goal, 'sufficiency' to deter is an adequate strategy; the quest for nuclear superiority must be rejected.
3. Nuclear deterrence should be used as a step on the way towards progressive disarmament.

In light of these general judgements we oppose some specific proposals in respect to our present deterrence posture:

1. The addition of weapons which are likely to be vulnerable to attack, yet also possess a 'prompt hard-target kill' capability that threatens to make the other side's retaliatory forces vulnerable. Such weapons may

seem to be useful primarily in a first strike. We resist such weapons for this reason and we oppose Soviet deployment of such weapons which generate fear of a first strike against US forces.

2. The willingness to foster strategic planning which seeks a nuclear war-fighting capability that goes beyond the limited function of deterrence outlined in this letter.
3. Proposals which have the effect of lowering the nuclear threshold and blurring the difference between nuclear and conventional weapons.

In support of the concept of 'sufficiency' as an adequate deterrent — we recommend:

1. Support for immediate, bilateral, verifiable agreements to halt the testing, production and deployment of new nuclear weapons systems.
2. Support for negotiated bilateral deep cuts in the arsenals of both superpowers, particularly those weapons systems which have destabilising characteristics.
3. Support for early and successful conclusion of negotiations of a comprehensive test ban treaty.
4. Removal by all parties of short-range nuclear weapons which multiply dangers disproportionate to the deterrent value.
5. Removal by all parties of nuclear weapons from areas where they are likely to be overrun in the early stages of war, thus forcing rapid and uncontrollable decision on their use.
6. Strengthening of command and control over nuclear weapons to prevent inadvertent and unauthorised use – any claim by any government that it is pursuing a morally acceptable policy of deterrence must be scrutinised with the greatest care. We are prepared and eager to participate in our country in the ongoing public debate on moral grounds ...

The Ethics of Nuclear Deterrence

Report of a Working Party of the Church of England

The ethics of deterrence are the ethics of threatening to do something which one believes would be immoral, which one intends to do only in circumstances which will not arise because of the conditional threat.

In analysing this issue we begin by noting that what is threatened is a response to aggression by means which we have already suggested cannot be morally acceptable. Such a conditional intention implies that one has consented in one's mind to act immorally.

But it may be said the West has not consented to act immorally, because it will never have to use its nuclear weapons. Two alternative reasons might support this supposition. One is that the threat to use nuclear weapons is a bluff. The other is that nuclear deterrence will succeed in keeping the peace indefinitely. It would be impossible in practice to maintain a bluff. But even if it were possible the policy would still be morally questionable. We are our brothers' keepers. Anyone who threatens to annihilate his opponents encourages them and others to respond in kind and bears some responsibility for the moral climate which prevails. To believe that a policy is immoral and at the same time encourage others to support it, train others to carry it through and argue down its opponents, would be morally and spiritually corrupt.

The other ground or a judgment that the West will never use nuclear weapons is the belief that nuclear deterrence will continue to keep the peace. Even if one accepts the presumption that it is the existence of nuclear weapons which has helped to keep the peace until now, how can one be certain that it will continue to do so?

It can be argued that the West has no intention of using its weapons unless an opponent attacks it, knowing that in that case the West will use its nuclear weapons. In such a case, it might be argued, the opponent would have to accept full moral responsibility for the West's response. This argument is unsound if Western nuclear weapons are used, it will be because of decisions the West will have taken and which will have been part of the chain of events leading to the deaths which follow. The moral dilemma cannot be avoided in the way suggested.

Our arguments seem to converge on the conclusion that even the possession and possible conditional intention to use nuclear weapons is itself immoral. Is there any way of avoiding this conclusion?

On the one hand there are those who think that to threaten to use nuclear weapons with all their dreadful effects and the attendant risk of nuclear holocaust, is utterly unacceptable, whatever might be the result of abandoning such a policy. On the other hand, there are those who think that the effect of abandoning nuclear deterrence is so frightening that, evil and risky though the deterrent policy may be, it is the least evil course at present available, until something better can be found...

If the deterrent is to work, you have to convince an enemy that you are willing to use it : but if you have to use it, it has failed.

From this trap there might seem one theoretical possibility of escape. Might not deterrence work if one threatened to use it but arranged secretly never to do so? This secret must be confined virtually to two or three top political leaders who, in a democratic society, might be replaced at any moment by others who did not share their views, and who could never be initiated into them in advance, because the matter could not be publicly debated. Furthermore, to keep up an effective deterrent both the public and the service would have to be constantly indoctrinated with the belief that use of nuclear weapons was in the last resort justified. In short, to have a nuclear arsenal deployed is to be committed already to using it in certain circumstances. Quite apart from the fact that it is morally questionable to threaten to use something it is wrong actually to use, it would in practice be impossible in this case to threaten to use it and not actually use it when the moment comes. Admittedly nerve might fail; use might not be considered necessary after all; but a purely moral restraint could not in practice be enforced.

The crucial point, proves to be this. There are no weapons whose effect will not be cataclysmic... can be used, particularly against the conventional force superiority of the Warsaw Pact countries, in an intermediate situation between ordinary war and disastrous holocaust.

If it is the very use of nuclear weapons which is morally unacceptable, then a nuclear arsenal can be justified only if it is both intended and likely to prevent such use. You may either decide for a nuclear component in deterrence, and risk nuclear war, or decide against it and risk the political and human consequences of blackmail and defeat by someone with fewer moral inhibitions. We consider then the nuclear element in deterrence is no longer a reliable or morally acceptable approach to the future of the world. This judgement is reinforced by the fact that an integral part of deterrence in practice is crisis management, which may mean in effect going to the brink while relying on fallible human judgement, operating under tremendous stress, to see you through. Given all these considerations, we believe that a nuclear component in deterrence is not sufficiently compelling to outweigh the huge moral imperatives against using nuclear weapons at all.

We believe that mutually stimulated paranoia is blinding all concerned to the way their opponent is in fact likely to behave. The prophecies of aggression are self-fulfilling prophecies. The paranoia is created and intensified by the very existence of the nuclear weapons themselves.

The United Kingdom should renounce its independent nuclear deterrent, for two reasons; in the hope of putting new life into the Non-Proliferation Treaty, by showing that at least one of the nuclear powers is prepared to take its obligations under this instrument seriously; second, to eliminate what we feel to be a destabilising element in the world situation; Britain's ambiguously separate centre of decision making on the use of nuclear weapons.

The UK should cancel the order for the Trident missile at once and phase out the Polaris missiles and submarines...

The UK's withdrawal from other nuclear weapons should be phased in the following order:-

(i) Weapons wholly or mainly of British manufacture.

(ii) US made depth bombs, missiles, and artillery under dual key.

(iii) US air and submarine base facilities, and the projected Cruise missiles from 1983.

The timetable for the implementation of this withdrawal, especially (ii) and (iii), is a matter for negotiation with Britain's allies, but the decision to undertake the whole process should be taken in the same single political operation.

The Church and the Bomb[2]

The two main motions passed by the General Synod during the debate on 'The Church and the Bomb' were :

Motion 1

That this Synod, recognising (a) the urgency of the tasks of making and preserving peace; (b) the extreme seriousness of the threat made to the world by contemporary nuclear weapons and the danger in the present international situation; (c) that it is not for the Church to determine strategy but rather to give moral lead to the nation:

1. Affirms that it is the duty of Her Majesty's Government and allied to maintain adequate forces to guard against nuclear blackmail and to deter nuclear and non-nuclear aggressors.
2. Asserts that the tactics and strategies of this country, and her NATO allies should be seen to be unmistakably defensive in respect of the countries of the Warsaw pact.
3. Judges that even a small-scale first use of nuclear weapons could never be morally justified in view of the high risk this would lead to full-scale nuclear warfare.
4. Believes that there is a moral obligation on all countries (including the members of NATO) publicly to foreswear the first use of nuclear weapons in any form.
5. Bearing in mind that many in Europe live in fear of nuclear catastrophe and that nuclear parity is not essential to deterrence, calls on Her Majesty's Government to take immediate steps in conjunction with her allies to further the principle embodied in this motion so as to

2 'The Church and the Bomb : Nuclear Weapons and Christian Conscience', in *Bulletin of Peace Proposals*, Ibid, p. 256. Motion passed by Church of England.

reduce progressively NATO's dependence on nuclear weapons and to decrease nuclear arsenals throughout the world.

Motion 2

That this Synod believes that indiscriminate mass destruction in war cannot be justified in the light of Christian teaching and exhorts the dioceses to study and pray about the issues raised in the report 'The Church and the Bomb', and particularly the theological and moral issues, so as to enable Christian people to make a more informed and committed contribution to the making and preserving of peace and to search for ways of resolving conflict other than by war.

The System of Nuclear Deterrence must not Dominate our common Future[3]

Statement by the Council of the Evangelical Church in Germany on the Peace Discussions in Autumn 1983: Hanover, September 17, 1983.

...We are convinced that the elements of joint security must be reinforced in face of the attempt to find security in confrontation. The system of nuclear deterrence and the boosting of weapons potentials must not dominate our common future. The EKD Council reiterates its urgent reminder that the crucial ethical and political goal remains that of safeguarding peace by political means and ending military confrontation and the nuclear arms race.

This demand required the readiness to take concrete steps. They could go in the following direction:

(a) The development, testing, production and stationing of more and more nuclear weapons as deterrence must not continue.

3 Ibid, pp. 257-258.

(b) The strategy of the West to prevent war must be further developed. The threat of the first use of nuclear weapons for defence against a conventional attack cannot remain its underlying principle, because the first use of weapons of mass destruction is intolerable for the Christian conscience.

(c) The goal of lessening the dangers inherent in the system of deterrence calls for the abandoning of rigid and categorical thinking about parity. This also applied to the consideration of whether single cases of unilateral disarmament... lead to the destabilisation of the balance of power or, smooth the way to negotiated results and thus have a stabilising effect.

(d) At the present moment the crucial thing is to lead Europe out of the threat of an escalation and new quality of arms build-up.

The prevention of war in any form does not, however, merely call for a change in military strategy. It must rely more and more strongly on political elements representing the accommodation and interlocking of interests.

Such elements are: economic cooperation, joint efforts to preserve nature and the basis for life on earth and joint efforts for a more just, less unstable world economic order. Connective strands must be retained and created, which neither side can cut without harm to itself. This can lead to an agreement on institutions, add procedures which reduce conflicts and contribute to crisis resolution. The goal remains that of worldwide peace order relying for its stability on less power and increasingly on the approval of the people and nations concerned.

2. To the Christians in positions of political responsibility:

...In its memorandum 'The Preservation, Promotion and Renewal of Peace' the EKD Council pointed out that latitude granted for the moment by mutual deterrence must be used to break through the chain of arms buildup, because otherwise the time will come when the scandal and risk of the arms race will have to be judged greater than the usefulness of deterrence.

The debate about the responsibility of the government and parliament for peace policy must be conducted in a spirit of courageous candour and clarity, as befits the significance of this problem. We ask all politicians to take the doubts and deep concern in the population seriously.

We especially ask the politicians not to suspect those resorting to means of political protest and legal, peaceful demonstration, but to acknowledge these as legitimate democratic expressions of opinion and to do their best so that demonstrations may remain peaceful.

...Whoever wants to safeguard external peace by political means must not sacrifice internal peace to violence.

To all those bearing responsibility in the church.

...The Church's message must be proclaimed in a sinful world needful of salvation. However, this does not mean that it should fatalistically accept the manmade threat of nuclear weapons or learn to live with it.

The ethical aim of a peace policy not based in deterrence is binding on all of us, even though the way to reach this goal is controversial in its specific details. We thus ask those with special responsibilities in the church not to abandon its fellowship, but to listen to one another and attach greater importance to prayer for peace and enlightenment on our common way forward than the pressure of opposing opinions which beset us in the church too.

The Maintenance of Peace[4]

Joint Pastoral Letter of the German Catholic Bishops

1. Security policy within the framework of peace policy.

There are chiefly two threats looming ahead: the danger to the freedom of nations and their citizens from totalitarian systems which disregard elementary human rights in their sphere of dominion and which might be remitted to use their power for expansion or for the application of political influence and extortion; the second danger lies in an escalation of armaments with an immense accumulation of nuclear and conventional weapons which. to the fear of many people, might one day cause the catastrophe of an outright war. We must counter both dangers simultaneously — above all by political means... An affirmation of military power as a component of security policy does not contradict the enunciated demand of settling conflicts by nonviolent methods. Today, military power must even primarily serve this objective. We must, therefore, consider what demands must today be made of such a military contribution and what criteria should govern it.

In the face of the other danger arising from the arms race, the important thing is to do everything which diminished the risks of an arms build-up in the interest of our joint survival without endangering one's own security. The threat and use of force must be removed, or at least gradually reduced in international relations.

Dangerous misconceptions and miscalculations can only be avoided if all sides are seriously and permanently willing to re-examine their own position at the same time to give due consideration the experience and anxiety, the interests, the perceptions and the values of the other side.

---

4 'Out of Justice, Peace : The Church in Service of Peace', Ibid, pp.269-271.

For that reason, the aim of the military contribution towards the maintenance of peace under present conditions must not lie in the waging of war but in the preventing of war and indeed of any warfare at all...

2. The prevention of war

Hitherto the attempt is being made to prevent war by means of their nuclear deterrent...

The following question arises: Under the system of mutual deterrence, can either side really be sure of his opponent's intentions?... Some of the standpoints which must be considered in an ethical judgement of the nuclear deterrent:

The first and decisive standpoint is the goal of this strategy, i.e. the prevention of war. If that is the goal of the deterrent according to the declared will of the politicians and strategists, then the political and military leaders must be able to substantiate the fact that war can really be prevented by this strategy and why they consider this to be the case ...

The second standpoint for an assessment of the deterrent thus refers to the means. i.e. the envisaged conventional and nuclear weapons as well the appropriate operational planning. The intention of preventing war with one's strength must become credible by virtue of the choice of the whole range of arms ...

If the deterrent is intended to establish above all a political objective for the chosen weapons within the framework of prevention of a war, then these must be judged primarily in these terms ...

These various points of view point to the criteria which a deterrence must satisfy if it is still to be acceptable in ethical terms.

2.1 Existing or planned military means must never render war more feasible or more probable : We clearly realise that this demand of ours will encounter opposition which can hardly be overcome. After all, weapons only provide an effective deterrent if their use can be threatened in a credible manner. The use of a threat of mass destruction which one must never carry out — a morally intolerable concept — is regarded as being particularly effective for the purpose of preventing war. This immense tension is only acceptable if the whole range of security policy is directed towards the goal of preventing war and if the military measures remain integrated within the higher ranking concept of 'maintaining peace by political means'.

2.2 Only such military means and so many military means may be deployed as are necessary for the purpose of the deterrent aimed at preventing war.

In particular, the military means must not indicate any quest for superiority. Rather, they must be geared to the objective of achieving stability, which then prevails when neither side can derive political or military benefit from their weapon systems. We must not in the long run satisfy ourselves with a minimum of destructive potential which is always fraught with a real danger of explosion (John Paul II). For that reason, all responsible persons in the State and in society have the urgent duty to strive with their whole strength towards finding alternatives to the threat of mass destruction.

2.3 All military means must be compatible with effective mutual arms limitation, arms reduction and disarmament.

So far, this goal has not been achieved...

A war of destruction is never a solution and never permissible. The fact that this possibility nevertheless exists shows that mankind is now in an impasse which forces us to act with courage. The only solution lies in undertaking greater efforts towards a political maintenance of peace and continuous disarmament. States and power blocs must finally learn to shape their relations without the threat or use of force.

Renunciation of the Spirit and Logic of Nuclear Deterrence[5]

Resolution of the Synod of the Federation of Protestant Churches in the German Democratic Republic:-

... We hope that this renunciation (of the spirit and logic of deterrence) will open the way to a more flexible policy that can gradually lead us out from the compulsions of the deterrence system and make possible a system of justice and common security between East and West, North and South. We see real opportunities today to translate (this) into concrete steps in the following:-

- a nuclear freeze.
- taking up the world disarmament campaign launched by the UN and making it apply to our own country.
- requesting our government to outlaw the use of nuclear weapons and the possession as a crime against humanity. (Vancouver : Declaration of Peace and Justice, Nov. 25)
- requesting our government to promote trust and cooperation in the interest of common security ...

...We hail the fact that the Chairperson of the Protestant leadership Conference in the GDR and the Chairperson of the Council of Protestant Church in (West) Germany, acting out of their churches' special responsibility, have addressed the governments of both German states with the plea that, within their respective alliances, do what they can to see that the negotiations in Geneva progress successfully and a palpable reduction of weapons systems on both sides be attained.

5 Ibid, pp. 262-263.

Hope Against Hope in the Nuclear Age[6]

A Pastoral Letter to all congregations by the General Synod of the Netherlands Reformed Church.

It is now eighteen years since the 1962 pastoral letter 'On the Question of Nuclear Weapons' was published in which the Synod uttered a 'No without any yes' to nuclear arms.

The Synod did not speak unambiguously about the possession of nuclear weapons. The reason for this was not because a qualifying clause was added to the 'No' which implied a 'Yes' to the deterrent function of nuclear weapons, but because 'abolition' of these weapons, was possible in the normal sense of the word...

On the contrary, the experience of the last eighteen years has shown us how the possession of these weapons can sweep us all or along in their accelerated build-up and sophistication and in the development of a strategy of 'limited' nuclear warfare. So, first of all, we must repeat our 'No' and then in all clarity state that this 'No' also holds without qualification for the possession of all nuclear weapons.

Of course we continue to hope for steps towards bilateral and multilateral disarmament. But at the same time we consider it necessary to plead for an approach in which negotiation goes hand in hand with steps which are already clearly set upon the road of disarmament; since it has turned out to be impossible to reach multilateral decisions leading towards such steps, they should be taken unilaterally. They should not only point out the direction to be taken; they should also testify to a readiness to take that road ourselves. We consider that the denuclearisation of the Netherlands would be such an unambiguous step.

In this present time of great danger for the whole of humanity, we look to the coming of him, who says to his

6 Ibid, pp. 264-265.

Church: Do not fear, I am the first and the last, and the living one; and I was dead, and behold, I am alive for evermore, and I have the keys of death (Rev. 1 : 17-18).

The Church and Peace[7]

Statement by the Bishops' Conference of the Church of Norway, Fredrikstad, 29 March - 2 April 1982.

3. The Church's responsibility for peace

More than anytime it is necessary that Christians today pray to God for help and rescue, in order that agony of war may be kept away from us.

4. Justice and Peace

The underlying causes for rearmament, conflict and war are numerous and complex. In this world of sin we will never be able to realise complete peace between man and nations. It is, therefore, also part of God's will that injustice shall be restrained by the power granted to political authorities. The Christian church regards these authorities as expressions of God's will that injustice shall be restrained by the power granted to political authorities. The Christian Church regards these authorities as expressions of God's will to uphold order and justice among men. On this basis, the church has also thought it right and justifiable to have sufficient military defence to guard a nation's freedom and rights. The church has also regarded it justifiable to uphold these rights by the use of military force, if necessary.

It is generally accepted, also in our church, that a military defence which is supposed to wage 'just wars', is ethically justifiable. This implies a defence aiming at restraining injustice and ward off an evil which puts the life and future of a people at stake.

---

7 Ibid, pp. 269-270.

...our church wants to protect the conscience of individuals who after serious considerations conclude that it is not ethically justifiable to serve in the armed forces.

The limits of war :

To start and fight out a war with these weapons is thus in a fundamental way a destruction of Creation itself. In such a situation the development of nuclear arms must be described as an expression of man's revolt against God. It is an abuse of knowledge and resources which according to God's will are meant for the benefit of all humankind.

The increasing rearmament, with its strains on the peoples, and the growing tension in the world, in many cases lead to the violation of basic human rights; fear and insecurity paralyse people. ...remove from them the possibility of a life in freedom and joy. We are witnessing nations being attacked and occupied, the freedom of opinion being subdued and individuals being interned or done away with.

Disarmament

This fear for the future is in itself a calamity for humankind, implying great ethical problems. Man must be liberated from the threat of a nuclear war. This does not mean that other mass weapons of a more conventional kind are more acceptable. But, disarmament must have a visual starting point in that states today having nuclear arms, or possessing the capacity to develop them, dispose off these weapons. ...together with Christians and churches all over the earth we appeal to the world's statesmen to sit down together, deliberately and immediately, in order to dispose off all arsenals of nuclear arms.

Appendix 2

STATEMENTS BY INTERNATIONAL CHURCH ORGANISATIONS

Statement on Peace and Justice by the Sixth General Assembly of the World Council of Churches , Vancouver, August 1983.[1]

1. The World Council of Churches has consistently drawn the attention of the churches to the economic threats to peace. Even without war, thousands perish daily in nations both rich and poor because of hunger and starvation.
2. While the equivalent of nearly two billion dollars (US) is being expended globally each day for armaments, the world economy is engulfed in a prolonged and deepening crisis which threatens every country and international security.

No Peace Without Justice

3. The peoples of the world stand in need of peace and justice. Peace is not just the absence of war, peace cannot be built on foundations of injustice. Peace requires a new international order based on justice for and within all the nations, and respect for the God-given humanity and dignity of every person. Peace is, as the Prophet Isaiah has taught us, the effect of righteousness.

1 *Buttetin of Peace Proposals* (1984).

4. From its inception, peace with Justice has been a central concern of the ecumenical movement.

Nuclear weapons and disarmament

The growing sophistication, accuracy and mobility of new generations to weapons now ready for deployment or currently being designed make them more dangerous and destabilizing than ever before. The failure of arms control among nuclear-weapon states has made the non-proliferation treaty, in practice, an instrument of invidious discrimination, incited the spread of nuclear weapons, and compounded the prospects for nuclear war in several areas of regional tension in the Southern hemisphere.

We call upon the churches, especially those in Europe, both East and West, and in North America, to redouble their efforts to convince their governments to reach a negotiated settlement and to turn away now - from plans to deploy additional or new nuclear weapons in Europe, and to ... immediately ... reduce and then eliminate altogether present nuclear forces.

We urge the churches as well to intensify their efforts to stop the rapidly growing deployment of nuclear weapons and support systems in the Indian and Pacific Oceans, and to press their governments to withdraw from or refuse to base service ships or airplanes bearing nuclear weapons in those regions.

5. The volume of highly profitable trade in conventional weapons has nearly doubled in the past five years, a very large part of it in the direction of the developing nations and regions where armed conflict already defies containment. The destructive power of these weapons steadily crosses the distinction between conventional and nuclear warfare:-

(a) Nuclear war can under no circumstances, in no region and by no social system be just or justifiable, given ...the magnitude of devastation caused by it will be far out of proportion to any conceivable benefit ...to be derived from it .

(b) Nuclear war is unlikely to remain limited.

(c) All nations now possessing nuclear weapons or capable of doing so in the foreseeable future should unequivocally renounce policies of 'first use' .

(d) The concept of deterrence, the credibility of which depends on the possible use of nuclear weapons, is to be rejected as morally unacceptable and as incapable of safeguarding peace and security in the long-term.

(e) The production and deployment of nuclear weapons as well as their use ...should be a complete halt in the production of nuclear weapons and in weapons research and development in all nations, to be expeditiously enforced through a treaty.

(f) All nations should agree to ratify a comprehensive test ban treaty.

(g) All means leading to disarmament, both nuclear and conventional, should be welcomed as complementary and mutually reinforcing multilateral ...bilateral ...unilateral initiatives leading to the relaxation of tension and building of mutual confidence among nations and peoples.

We urge the churches to press their government to abstain from any further research, production or deployment of weapons in space, and to prohibit the development and production of all weapons of mass destruction ...including chemical and biological.

Peace, Justice and Common Security[2]

Message of the Christian World Conference, Life and Peace Uppsala (Sweden), 20-23 April, 1983.

1. The Christian concern for life and peace.

...The Christian gospel is a gospel of peace. From the beginning that gospel has been preached in a violent world. Today, however, we witness violence real or potential, on an unprecedented scale. For the first time in history we human beings, always possessed of limited power to destroy, are now capable of wiping out the civilisation for centuries. The production and threat to use nuclear weapons capable of annihilating the human race demonstrates an ultimate arrogance before God who alone disposes off... life and death....

We confess that we have not always called war into question as a means of settling conflicts.

2. The doctrine of nuclear deterrance. The current military and political doctrine of nuclear deterrence must be challenged. The dangers of nuclear proliferation and accident, and the increasing sophistication of weaponry, leading to the concept of the so-called 'limited nuclear war', all render the doctrine of nuclear deterrence increasingly dubious and dangerous from every point of view. From the Christian stand-point reliance upon the threat and possible use of nuclear weapons is unacceptable as a way of avoiding war. Some are willing to tolerate nuclear deterrence only as a temporary measure in the absence of alternatives.

3. Common security. The security of one nation cannot be achieved by endangering the security of others or by seeking military superiority over others. The devising of an alternative international security system based on

2 Ibid, p.278-280.

the principle of common security, and resolute steps towards disarmament should go hand in hand.

4. The arms trade. The international arms trade is sinister, clinical and unprincipled. Its growth has gone hand-in-hand with the increase in the number of oppressive military regimes, which violate human rights and foster injustice. It has also provided the munitions for the scores of wars fought mainly on Third World soil since the last world war. This trade must be condemned and internationally controlled.

Statement on Peace

By the Lutheran World Federation Executive Committee, Turku. Finland, 4-13 August 1981.

The Executive Committee affirms

5. ...that Christians have a responsibility to seek peaceful means for resolving political conflicts and for eliminating injustices and oppression, recognising that the choices presented are often between greater or lesser evils; and
6. ...consult with each other regarding church actions supporting peace, disarmament, nonproliferation of nuclear weapons, support of negotiations and the pursuit of human rights. Social justice and national independence;
7. ...communicate to governments, political leaders and the wider public the churches' concern and efforts for peace.

Attention should be drawn especially to:

...the need for immediate action to reduce the threat of nuclear war:

the effort and experiences of churches in their work for peace in other countries and especially those living under different social systems ...

Appendix 3

JOHN PAUL II AND NON-VIOLENCE[1]

VIMAL TIRIMANNA

Keeping very much in line with his immediate predecessors and the Council, Pope John Paul II seems to be adopting what one may tend to call "a pacifist attitude" towards war. If there is any marked difference between the present Pope and his immediate predecessors, it is his consistency in adopting pacifist attitudes. Ever since the beginning of this papacy, John Paul had been consistently calling people to abandon war and violence in resolving international disputes and internal problems of nations.

The Pope's position on war and violence has been very clear almost from the very beginning of his papacy. For him "Violence only begets violence." "The Pope combined condemnation of social injustice with apparent support for a pacifist response to injustice."

The invasion of Kuwait by Iraqi forces on 2 August, 1991, certainly created a situation of injustice and the Pope did not hesitate to condemn it as "a violation of international law". Yet the Papal statements of that period regarding the crisis never justified the use of force or violence to correct this unjust

---

1. *Vidyajyoti Theological Review* (June 1993), pp. 1-7.

situation which upheld the use of limited force or violence on such occasions, under strict conditions ("Just war" criteria).

The first six months after the invasion of Kuwait, saw more than fifty papal statements on the Gulf crisis. However, in those statements one cannot find "definitive guidance for conscience" pleas and some principles. Nevertheless, as Bryan Hehir points out, there is a clear structure of argument running through all these statements.

Hehir considers the Pope's letter to President Bush in January, 1991 as the most clearly structured papal statement on the Gulf War.

"I wish now to state my firm belief that it is not likely to bring an adequate solution to international problems and that... the consequences that would possibly derive from war would be devastating and tragic."

One should note here the structure of the argument, which while acknowledging a "just cause", refuses to "justify" resort to force. The argument "rests on fears of disproportionate results".

The consistency of the present Pope's views on war and peace is seen once again after the Gulf war in his encyclical Centesimus Annus. His consistent non-violent position becomes apparent when he says:

"May people learn to fight for justice without silence, renouncing class struggle in their internal disputes, and war in international ones."

One needs first of all to address these root causes of war, if war is to be abolished. This, for the Pope, is a reason why the use of force is not the means to correct an unjust situation, for it creates further evil effects.

The eminent American theologian John Courtney Murray described in the early 1960s the Catholic position on war as fulfilling a triple function when he wrote:

"...To condemn war as evil, to limit the evil it entails, and to humanize its conduct as far as possible."

However, Pope John Paul II places much more emphasis on the condemnation of war than on efforts to limit its effects and humanize its conduct. He appears to be pessimistic about the ability to contain modern warfare. He stops just short of an absolute advocacy of non-violence. This "pacifist" position of the Pope is consistent throughout.

The Pope's opposition to war and violence is based mainly on his considerations of the consequences. For Yoder, we have to be non-violent because God is non-violent.

In Centesimus Annus, the Pope seems to put forward the experiences of Eastern Europe in the recent past as normative for all other situations as well. But the context of Eastern Europe was totally different from most of the other situations where people are clamouring for change and justice. It is naive to imagine that the same combination of factors for social change would ever exist in other situations that long for social change.

Bibliography

Primary Sources

- **Congressional Hearings.** *US-Soviet Strategic Policies* (March 1974). Briefing on Counterforce Attacks (September 1974).
- **International Encylopaedia of Social Sciences.** Brody, Richard, "Deterrence", Vol.4, pp.130-133.
  - Huntington, Samuel, "Millitary Policy", Vol.10, p.322.
- **National Conference of Catholic Bishops.** *Human Life in Our Day,* November 16, 1968 (Washington DC: US Catholic Conference, 1976).
  - National Institute for Public Policy, *Rationale and Requirements for U.S. Nuclear Forces and Arms Control,* Vol I, Executive Report (January 2001),12.
- **Speeches and Press Conference**. Dulles, John Foster, "The Evolution of Foreign Policy", *Department of State Bulletin* XXX, January 25, 1954.
  - Ikle Fred C., "Prevention of War in a World of Uncertainty", *Department of State Bulletin,* 70, March 25, 1974, pp.311-318.
  - Kissinger, Henry, "The Western Alliance: Peace and Moral Purpose", *Department of State Bulletin,* 75 (July 26, 1976), p.110.

- **United Nations Publications.** "A Periodic Review: START and Beyond", Vol.15, United Nations, No.2 (New York: UN, 1992), pp.9-31.
  - Department of Disarmament Affairs, Vol. 11 (New York: UN, 1987) & Vol. 17 (1992).
  - "New Realities: Disarmament, Peace Building and Global Security", (New York: UN, 1993).
  - Asia-Pacific Region: Non-Proliferation and Other Disarmament Issues (New York: UN,1991).
  - UN Topical Papers on Disarmament, No.8 (Fall 1991).
- Wireless File."U.S. Detargets All Strategic Nuclear Missiles", *Backgrounder,* Defense Department Report, June 1, 1994 (New Delhi: USIS, 1994).
- "The Challenge of Peace: God's Promise and Our Response", Catholic National Conference report reproduced in *Strategic Digest* November 9, 1983, pp.691-745.
- *Gaudium et Spes* in Abbott and J Gallagher (eds) *The Documents of Vatican II* (London: Geoffrey Chapman, 1966).
- Augustine Aurelius, *The City of God trans* J. Healey (London, 1945), also by Dodd Marcus (New York: Modern Library, 1950).
- Clausewitz, Carl Von, *On War* trans Michael Howard and Peter Paret (Princeton, NJ: Princeton University Press, 1976).
- John XXIII, *Pacem in Terris* (New York: America Press, 1963).
- Yzermans, Vincent A.,(ed.), *The Major Address of Pope Pius XII,* Vol.II (St. Paul's: North Central Publishing Co., 1961).

Secondary Sources

- Abel, Ellis, *The Missile* Crisis (New York: Bantam Books, 1966).
- Aldridge, Robert C., *First Strike!: Pentagon's Strategy for Nuclear War* (Boston : South End Press, 1983).
- Allers, Ulrich S., and O'Brien, William W., (eds.), *Christian Ethics and the Nuclear Warfare* (Washington; Institute of World Policy: Georgetown University, 1961).
- Allison, Graham T., *Essence of Decision: Explaining the Cuban Missile* Crisis (Boston: Little Brown, 1971).
- — do —, Carnesale, Albert, & Nye, Joseph S. Jr., (eds.), *Hawks Doves Owls: An Agenda for Avoiding Nuclear War* (New York; Norton,1985).
- — do —, and Traverton Gregory F., (eds.), *Rethinking America's Security: Beyond Cold War to New World Order* (New York & London: W.W.Norton & Company, 1992).
- — do — and Carter A.B., Miller, S.E., and Zelikon, P., (eds.), *Cooperative Denuclearization: From Pledges to Deeds,* Harvard Project on Cooperative Denuclearization (CSIA: Harvard, 1993).
- Ambrose, Stephen E., *Rise to Globalism: America's Foreign Policy,* 1938-1980 (New York: Penguin Books, 1980).
- Anderson, Annelise and Bark, Dennis L., (eds.), *Thinking About America: The United States in the 1990s* (Stanford, CA.: Hoover Institution Press, 1988).
- Aquinas, Thomas, *Summa Theologica,* 3 volumes (New York: Benizger Brothers, 1912-1922).
- Aristotle, *Nicomachean Ethics* (New York: Merrill, 1962).

- Aaron, Raymond, *The Century of Total* War (New York, Garden City: Doubleday Company, 1954).
- *— do —, History and the Dialectic of Violence - An Analysis of Satre's Critique De La Raison Dialectic,* trans Barry Cooper (Oxford:Basil Blackwell, 1975).
- *— do —, Peace and War,* trans. by Howard and Annuity, Baker Fox (New York: Praeger, 1968).
- Art, Robert and Waltz,. K. (eds.), *The Use of Force: Military Power and International Politics* (New York & London, Lanham: University Press of America, 1988).
- Bainton, Roland, H., *Christian Attitudes Towards War and Peace: A Historical Survey and Critical Re-evaluation* (New York, Nashville: Abingdon Press, 1960).
- Ball, Desmond, *Politics and Force Levels - The Strategic Missile Program and the Kennedy Administration* (Berkeley: University of California Press, 1980).
- Bark, Dennis L.,(ed.), *To Promote Peace: US Foreign Policy in the Mid 1980s* (Stanford University, CA: Hoover Institution Press,1985).
- Barnet, Richard J., *Real Security: Restoring American Power in a Dangerous Decade* (New York: Touchstone Books, 1981)
- Baylis, J., et. al., *Contemporary Strategy: Theories and Policies* (London: Croom Helm Ltd., 1975).
- *— do —,* & Garnett, John (eds.), *Makers of Nuclear Strategy* (London: Pinter 1991).
- Beauchamp, Tom L., *Philosophical Ethics: An Introduction to Moral Philosophy* (New York: McGraw Hill, 1992).
- Beaufre, Andre, *Deterrence and Strategy,* trans Major General R.H. Barry (New York: Praeger, 1966)

- Beilenson, Lawrence, *Survival and Peace in the Nuclear Age* (Chicago: Regnery Gateway Inc., 1980).
- Bennet, John C.,(ed.), *Nuclear Weapons and the Conflict of Conscience* (New York : Charles Scribners Sons, 1962).
- *— do —, Apocalypse* (Chicago: University of Chicago Press, 1980).
- Bernstein, Barton J., (ed.), *The Atomic Bomb: The Critical Issues* (Boston: Little Brown, 1976).
- Betts, Richard K., *Surprise Attack* (Washington: Brookings, 1982).
- Blackett, M.S., *Fear, War and the Bomb* (New York: Whitewalls House, 1948).
- Blainey, Geoffrey, *The Causes of War* (New York: Free Press, 1973).
- Blair, Bruce, *Strategic Command and Control: Redefining the Nuclear Threat* (Washington : Brookings Institution, 1985) .
- Blake, Nigel and Pole, Kay, *Dangers of Deterrence: Philosophers on Nuclear Strategy* (London and Boston: Routledge and Kegan Paul, 1983).
- — do —, *Objections to Nuclear Defense: Philosophers on Deterrence* (London: Routledge and Kegan Paul, 1984).
- Bobrow, Davis, (ed.), *Components of Defense Policy* (Chicago: Rand McNally, 1965).
- Booth, Ken, *Strategy and Ethnocentrism* (London : Croom Helm, 1973).
- Borden, William, *There Will Be No Time* (New York: Macmillan, 1946).

- Boulding, Kenneth., E., *Conflict and Defense: A General Theory* (New York: Harper and Row, 1963).
- Bozemann, Adda B., *Selected Essays: Strategic Intelligence and Statecraft* (New York: Brasseys, 1992).
- Bracken, Paul, *The Command and Control of Nuclear Forces* (New Haven, Conn.: Yale University Press, 1983).
- Briton, Abbott A., and Landhewr, Stephanie J., *The Politics of War and Peace: A Survey of Thought* (Washington: University Press of America, 1981).
- Brennan, Donald, (ed.), *Arms Control, Disarmament and National Security* (New York: George Braziller, 1961).
- Bridge, F., *The Cross and the Bomb* (Mowbray: Oxford University Press, 1983).
- Brodie, Bernard, *The Absolute Weapon: Atomic Power and World Order* (New York: Harcourt Brace, 1946).
- — do —, *From Crossbow to H-Bomb: The Evolution of Weapons and The Tactics of Warfare* (Bloomington: Indiana University Press, 1973).
- — do —, *War and Politics* (London: Macmillan 1973).
- — do —, *Strategy in the Missile Age* (Princeton, N.J.: Princeton University Press, 1970).
- Brown, Anthony, *Dropshot: The American Plan for World War III with Russia (Soviet Union) in 1957* (New York: Dial Press / James Wade, 1978).
- Brown, Harold, *Thinking About National Security* (Boulder, Colorado: Westview Press, 1983).
- Brown, Michael E., *Deterrence Failures and Deterrence Strategies* (Santa Monica : RAND Corporation, 1977).

- Bundy, McGeorge, *Danger and/or Survival: Choices About the Bomb in the First Fifty Years* (New York: Random House, 1988).
- Brzezinski, Zbignew K., *Out of Control: Global Turmoil on the Eve of the Twenty First Century* (New York: Charles Scribner's, 1993).
- Butterfield, Herbert, *Christianity and History* (London: Fortune Books, 1949).
- Campbell, John C., *The U.S. in World Affairs. 1948-49* (New York: Harper, 1949).
- Carnesale, Albert, Doty, Paul, Hoffmann, Stanley, Huntington, Samuel,Nye, Joseph and Sagan, Scott, *Living With Nuclear Weapons*, Harvard Study Group(Cambridge, Harvard University Press, 1983).
- Carpenter, Thomas Boyd, *Conventional Deterrence in the 1990s* (UK: Royal United Service Institute for Defense Studies/Macmillan, 1989).
- Carter, Ashton B, Perry, H. and Steinbrunner, J., *A New Concept of Cooperative Security* (Washington: Brookings Occasional Papers, 1992).
- Carver, Field Marshal, *A Policy for Peace* (London: Faber & Faber, 1982).
- Castelli, Jim, *The Bishops and the Bomb: Waging Peace in the Nuclear Age* (New York : Doubleday, 1983).
- Catudal, Honore M., *Nuclear Deterrence: Does it Deter?* (New York: Mansell Publications Ltd., 1985).
- Cheshire, Leonard, Gp. Capt., *The Light of Many Suns* (London: Methane, 1985).
- Childress, James E., *Moral Responsibility in Conflicts: Essays on Non Violence, War and Conscience* (Baton Rouge & London: Louisiana State University Press, 1982).

- Churchill, Winston, *The Grand Alliance* (Boston: Houghton-Mifflin, 1950).
- Cimbala, Stephen J., *Strategy After Deterrence* (New York: Praeger, 1991).
- — do —, *Force and Diplomacy in the Future* (New York: Praeger, 1992).
- Chilton, P., (ed.), *Language and the Nuclear Arms Debate: Nukespeak Today* (London: Francis Pinter, 1985).
- Donagan, Allen, *The Theory of Morality* (Chicago: University of Chicago Press, 1977).
- Dougherty, James and Pfaltzgraff, Robert Jr., *Contending Theories of International Politics* (Philadelphia, P.A: J.B Lippincott, 1971).
- — do, et. al —, *Ethics, Deterrence and National Security* (Washington DC: Pergamom Brassey, 1985).
- Douglas, James, *The Non-Violent Cross: A Theology of Revolutions and Peace* (New York : Macmillan, 1979).
- Douhet, Guilio, *The Command of the Air, trans.* Dino Ferraro (New York: Howard McCann Inc., 1942).
- Dyson, Freeman, *Weapons and Hope* (New York: Harper & Row, 1984)
- — do —, *Infinite in all Directions* (New York: Harper & Row 1988/Perennial Library edn., 1989).
- Earle, Edward Mead, *Makers of Modern Strategy* (New York: Athenaeum, 1966).
- Eden, Lynn, Miller Steven E., *Nuclear Argument: Understanding the Strategic Nuclear Arms and Arms Control Debate* (Ithaca: Cornell University Press, 1989).

- Eliot, George Fielding, *Victory Without Wars – 1958-61* (Annapolis, Md:U.S Naval Institute, 1958).
- Enthoven, Alain C. and Smith, Wayne K., *How Much Is Enough: Shaping the Defense Program – 1961- 1969* (New York: Harper & Row, 1971)
- Erickson, John (ed.), *The Military Technical Revolution: Its Impact on Strategy and Foreign Policy* (New York: Institute for the Study of USSR, 1966)
- Falk, Richard, *Law, Morality and War in the Contemporary World* (New York: Praeger Publishers, 1963).
- — do —, *A Study of Future Worlds* (New York: Macmillan: The Free Press, 1975).
- — do —, Kolko, Gabriel, and Lifton, R.J., (eds.), *Crimes of War* (New York: Random House, 1971).
- . — do — and Lifton, Robert Jay, *Indefensible Weapons: The Political and Psychological Case Against Nuclearism* (New York: Basic Books, 1982).
- Feeney, Margaret M., *Sword of the Spirit: Just War? Papal Teaching on Nuclear Warfare with a Scientific Commentary* (Hinkley, Leicestershire: Walker, 1958).
- Finletter, Thomas, *Power and Policy* (New York: Harcourt and Brace, 1940).
- Finnis, John M., Boyle, J.M. Jr. and Grissez G., *Nuclear Deterrence, Morality and Realism* (Oxford: Clarendon Press, 1988).
- Finnis, John M., *Fundamentals of Ethics* (Oxford: Clarendon Press, 1983).
- Fisher, D.R., *Morality and the Bomb* (London: Croom Helm, 1985).

- Fisher, Roger (ed.), *International Conflict and Behavioral Science* (New York: Basic Books, 1979).
- Ford, Harold and Winters F. X., S.J. (eds.), *Ethics and Nuclear Strategy* (New York: Maryknoll, 1985).
- Fox, William, *Atomic Energy and International Relations* (Mimeo: Yale Institute of International Affairs, 1948).
- Fox, Michael Allen and Goarke, Leo (eds.), *Nuclear War: Philosophical Perspectives* (New York: Peter Lang, 1985).
- Frank, Jerome, *Sanity* (Englewood Cliffs, N.J.: Prentice Hall, Random House, 1967).
- Frankena, William K., *Ethics* (Englewood Cliffs, N.J.: Prentice Hall, 1973).
- Freedman, Lawrence, *The Evolution of Nuclear Strategy* (London: Macmillan, 1981 and St Martin's Press, 1983).
- Fulbright, William J., *Old Myths and New Realities* (New York: Vintage, 1964).
- Fuller, J.F.C., *The Conduct of War – 1789-1961* (New York: Funk and Wagnels Co., 1961).
- Fussell, Paul, *The Great War and Modern Memory* (New York/London: Oxford University Press, 1975).
- Futrell, Robert F., *Ideas, Concepts, Doctrine: A History of Basic Thinking in the U.S Air Force: 1907-1964, Vol. II* (Maxwell Air Force Base, Ala.: Aerospace Studies Institute, 1971).
- Gaddis, John Lewis, *Strategies of Containment: A Critical Appraisal of Post War American National Security Policy* (New York: Oxford University Press, 1982).
- Galois, Pierre, *The Balance of Terror: Strategy for the Nuclear Age,* trans. Richard Howard (Boston: Houghton-Miffin, 1961).

- Garden, Timothy, Grp Capt., *Can Deterrence Last?: Peace Through a Nuclear Strategy* (London: Buchan and Enright Publishers, 1984).
- Garnett, John, *Theories of Peace and Security: A Reader in Contemporary Strategic Thought* (New York: Macmillan, 1979).
- Garthoff, Raymond L., *Soviet Military Doctrine* (Illinois: The Free Press, 1983).
- — do —, *Soviet Strategy in the Nuclear Age* (New York: Praeger, 1958).
- Generals for Peace and Diasarmament, *A Challenge to US/NATO Strategy* (New York: Universe Books, 1984).
- George, Alexander, Hall, David and Simmons, William, *The Limits of Coercive Diplomacy* (Boston: Little Brown, 1971).
- George, A. and Smoke, R., *Deterrence in American Foreign Policy: Theory and Practice* (New York: Colombia University Press, 1974).
- Gessert, Robert A. and Hehir, Bryan J., *The New Nuclear Debate* (New York: Council of Religious and International Affairs, 1976).
- Geyer, Alan, *The Idea of Disarmament: Rethinking the Unthinkable* (Elgin Ill: The Brethren Press, 1982).
- Giovanniti, Len and Freed, Fred, *Decision to Drop the Bomb* (New York: Coward McCann, 1965).
- Goodwin, Geoffrey (ed.), *Ethics and Nuclear Deterrence* (London: Croom Helm, 1981).
- Gottfried, Kurt and Blair, Bruce G.,(eds.), *Stability and Nuclear War* (New York: Oxford University Press, 1988).

- Graebner, Z., *Ideas and Diplomacy: Reading in the Intellectual Tradition of American Foreign Policy* (New York: Oxford University Press, 1964).
- Gray, Colin S., *Nuclear Strategy and Strategic Planning* (Phila, P.A.: Foreign Policy Research Institute, 1984).
- Green, Philip, *Deadly Logic: The Theory of Nuclear Deterrence* (Colombia: Ohio University Press, 1966).
- Greenwood, Ted, *Making the MIRV : A Study of Defence Decision Making* (Cambridge: Ballinger Publishing Co., 1975).
- Grisez, Germain and Shaw, Russell, *Beyond the New Morality* (Notre Dame: University of Notre Dame Press, 1974).
- Groves, Leslie R., *Now It Can Be Told: The Story of the Manhattan Project*(New York: Harper, 1962).
- Guertner, Gary L., *Deterrence and Defense in the Post Nuclear World* (New York: St Martin's Press, 1990).
- Gulley, Bill, *Breaking Cover* (New York: Warner Books, 1980).
- Halperin, Morton, *Defense for the Seventies,* 2nd Edition (Boston: Little Brown & Co., 1971).
- — do —, *Limited War in the Nuclear Age* (New York: John Wiley & Sons 1963).
- Hammond, Paul Y., *Organizing for Defense: The American Military Establishment in the Twentieth Century*(Princeton: Princeton University Press, 1961).
- Hardin, Russell, Mearsheimer, John J., Dworkin, Gerald and Goodwin, Robert E.,(eds.), *Nuclear Deterrence: Ethics and Strategy* (Chicago: University of Chicago Press,1985).

- Harkabi, Y., *Nuclear War Nuclear Peace* (Jerusalem: Israel Program for Scientific Translations, 1966).
- Harries, Rev. Richard, *What Hope in an Armed World?* (London: Pickering, 1982).
- Hart, B.H.Liddell, *History of the Second World War* (New York: Putnam, 1972).
- — do —, *Strategy: The Indirect Approach* (London: Faber & Faber, 1968).
- Held, V., Morgenbesser S., and Nagel, T., *Philosophy, Morality and International Affairs* (New York: Oxford University Press, 1974)
- Heike, Gregg, *The Winning Weapon: The Bomb in the Cold War, 1945-1950* (New York: Knopf, 1974).
- Hertz, J.H., *Political Realism and Political Idealism* (Chicago: University of Chicago Press, 1951).
- Heyer, Robert (ed.), *Nuclear Dilemma: Key Statements of Popes, Bishops, Councils and Churches* (New York: Paulist Press, 1982).
- Hewlett, Richard G. & Duncan Francis, *History of United States Atomic Energy Commission. Vol.II: Atomic Shield. 1947-1952* (University Park, Penn: State University Press, 1969).
- Hoffman, Stanley, *Primacy of World Order* (New York: McGraw Hill, 1981).
- — do —, *Duties Beyond Borders: On the Limits and Possibilities of Ethical International Politics* (Syracuse: Syracuse University Press, 1981).
- Hollenbach, David S.J., *Nuclear Ethics: A Christian Moral Argument* (New York: Paulist Press, 1983).
- Howard, Michael, (ed), *Restraints on War: Studies in the Limitation of Armed Conflict* (Oxford: Oxford University Press, 1979).

- — do —, *The Causes of War* (London: Unwin Hyman 1984).
- Huntington, Samuel P., *The Common Defense* (New York: Colombia University Press, 1961).
- — do —, *The Strategic Imperative: New Policies for American Security* (Cambridge: Ballinger, 1982).
- Huth, Paul, *Extended Deterrence and the Prevention of War* (New Haven: Yale University Press, 1989).
- Janis, Irving, *Victims of Groupthink: A Psychological Study of Foreign Policy, Decisions and Fiascoes* (Boston: Houghton-Mifflin & Co., 1972).
- — do —, *The Logic of Images in International Politics* (Princeton: Princeton University Press, 1962).
- Jervis, R., *Between Peace and War* (Baltimore : John Hopkins University Press,1981).
- Jervis, R., *Perception and Misperception in International Politics* (Princeton: Princeton University Press, 1976).
- Jervis, R., Lebow,R.N,.& Gross Stein, J.,(eds,), *Psychology and Deterrence* (Baltimore : John Hopkins University Press, 1985).
- — do —, *The Meaning of the Nuclear Revolution: Statecraft and the Prospect of Armageddon* (Ithaca: Cornell University Press, 19s89).
- Johnson, James Turner, *Ideology, Reason and Limitations of War* (Princeton, N.J.: Princeton University Press, 1981).
- — do —, *Just War Tradition and the Restraint of War* (Princeton, NJ : Princeton University Press,1981).
- — do —, *Can Modern War Be Just?* (New Haven, Conn: Yale University Press, 1984).

- Jones, Roy E., *Nuclear Deterrence: A Short Political Analysis* (London: Routledge & Kegan Paul,1968).
- Kahn, Jerome H., *Security in the Nuclear Age: Developing US Strategic Arms Policy* (Washington D.C.: Brookings Institution, 1975).
- Kahn, Herman, *Thinking About the Unthinkable* (New York: Horizon Press,1962).
- — do —, *On Thermonuclear War* (Princeton, N.J.: Princeton University Press, 1960).
- — do —, *On Escalation: Metaphors and Scenarios* (New York: Praeger, 1965).
- Kaplan, Fred, *The Wizards of Armageddon* (New York: Simon & Schuster,1983).
- Kaplan, Morton A.(ed.), *Strategic Thinking and Its Moral Implications* (Chicago: University of Chicago Press, 1973).
- Kaufmann, William, *W. (ed.), Military Policy and National Security (Princeton, NJ: Princeton University Press, 1956)*
- — do —, *The Requirements of Deterrence* 1-22 (Princeton, N.J.: Center for International Studies, Memorandum No. 7, 1954).
- — do —, *Military Policy and National Security* (Princeton: Princeton University Press,1956).
- — do —, *Decisions for Defense: Prospects for New Order* (Washington D.C.: Brookings Institution, 1991).
- Kegley, Charles & McGovern,Patrick (eds.), *Foreign Policy: USA/USSR* (Beverly Hills: SAGE Publications, 1982).
- Kelleher, Catherine, McArdle, Kerr, Frank J., Quester George H., (eds.), *Nuclear Deterrence: New Risks,*

New Opportunities (Washington: Pergamom-Brassey, 1986).

- Kennan, George F., *Memoirs 1925- 1950* (Boston: Little Brown, 1976).
- — do —, *The Nuclear Delusion: Soviet-American Relations in the Atomic Age* (London: Hamish Hamilton, 1984).
- Kennedy, E. M., et al., *Freeze: How To Prevent Nuclear War* (New York: Bantam Books, 1982).
- Kennedy, Paul, *Rise and Fall of Great Empires: Economic Change and Military Conflict from 1500 to 2000* (London: Unwin Hyman,1988).
- — do —, *Strategy and Diplomacy* (London: George Allen & Unwin, 1983).
- Kennedy, Robert, *Thirteen Days: A Memoir of the Cuban Missile Crisis* (New York: W.W. Norton & Co., 1969).
- Kenny, Anthony, *The Logic of Deterrence* (Chicago: University of Chicago Press, 1984).
- Keohane Robert, *After Hegemony* (Princeton N.J.: Princeton University Press,1984).
- Keohane, R.O. and Nye, Joseph, *Power and Interdependence: World Politics in Transition* (Boston: Little Brown & Co., 1977).
- Kirkpatrick, Jeane, J., *The Reagan Phenomenon and Other Speeches on Foreign Policy* (Washington: American Enterprise Institute for Public Policy Research,1983).
- Kissinger, Henry, A., *Nuclear Weapons and Foreign Policy* (New York, Garden City: Doubleday, 1958).

- — do —, *American Foreign Policy: Three Essays* (New York: W. W. Norton & Co., 1974).
- — do —, *Problems of National Strategy: A Book of Reading* (New York: Praeger, 1965).
- Knorr, Klaus, *On the Uses of Military Power in the Nuclear Age* (Princeton, N.J.: Princeton University Press, 1966).
- Kosinski, Jerry, *Being There* (London: Black Swan Books, 1970).
- Khrushchev, Nikita, *Khrushchev Remembers, Vol.II* (Boston: Little Brown & Co. 1970).
- Lackey, Douglas, *Moral Principles and Nuclear Weapons* (Totowa, N.J.: Roman & Allanheld, 1984).
- LaFeber, Walter, *America, Russia and the Cold War: 1945-1980.* 4th edn.(New York: John Wiley & Sons 1980).
- — do — (ed.), *The Dynamics of World Power: A Documentary History of US Foreign Policy 1945-1973* (New York: McGraw Hill Publication, 1973)
- Lebow, Richard Ned, *Between Peace and War: The Nature of International* Crisis (Baltimore: John Hopkins University Press, 1981).
- Lee, Steven, *Morality, Prudence and Nuclear Warfare* (N.Y: Cambridge University Press, 1993).
- Lefever, Earnest, W. (ed.), *Ethics and World Politics* (Baltimore: John Hopkins University Press, 1972).
- — do — & Hunt, Stephen, E., (ed.), *The Apocalyptic Premise: Nuclear Arms Debated* (Washington: Ethics & Public Policy Center, 1982).
- Lemmer, George,F., *The Air Force and Strategic Detente: 1951-1960* (Washington D.C.: Office of Air Force History, 1980).

- Levi, Warner, *The Coming End of War* (Beverly Hills CA:Sage,1981).
- Levine, Robert, *The Arms Debate* (Cambridge: Harvard University Press, 1963).
- Lille, Robert,D., *Organizing for Strategic Planning: The National System and the Air Force* (Washington DC: USAF Historical Division Liaison Office, April 1964).
- Long, Edward Leroy Jr., *War and Conscience in America* (Philadelphia: Westminster Press, 1968).
- Lillienthal, David Eli, *The Journals of David E. Lillienthal, Vol.II.* "The Atomic Years: 1945-50" (New York: Harper & Row, 1964)
- Lockwood, Jonathan S., *The Soviet View of US Strategic Doctrine* (New Brunswick, NJ: Oxford Transaction Books, 1983)
- Luckman,Thomas, *The Invisible Religion* (New York: Macmillan, 1967).
- Luttwak, Edward N., *Strategy and History: Collected Essays, Vol. II* (New Brunswick, NJ:Oxford Transaction Books, 1985).
- Little, Bradford, *The Flaw in Deterrence* (Chicago: Mid-West Pacifist Publishing Center,1983).
- Machiavelli, Nicolo, *The Prince,* trans. Robert Adams (New York: W.W. Norton, 1977).
- Mackie, J.L., *Ethics: Inventing Right and Wrong* (London: Penguin, 1977).
- Maclean, Douglas,(ed.), *The Security Gamble: Deterrence Dilemmas in the Nuclear Age* (Maryland Studies in Public Philosophy, Totowa, N.J.: Roman & Allanheld, 1984).

- Mandelbaum, Michael, *The Nuclear Question: United States and Nuclear Weapons 1946-1976* (Oxford: Cambridge University Press,1979).
- — do —, *The Nuclear Revolution* (Oxford: Cambridge University Press, 1981).
- — do —, *The Nuclear Future* (Ithaca: Cornell University Press, 1983).
- Martin, Lawrence (ed.), *Strategic Thought in the Nuclear Age* (London: Heinemann, 1979).
- Mathews, Lloyd J., & Brown, E. (eds.), *The Parameters of Military Ethics* (Washington: Pergamom Brassey, 1989).
- May, Earnest R., *Lessons of the Past* (New York: Oxford University Press,1973).
- May, Michael M. & Bing, George F. , Steinbrunner, John D., *Strategic Arms Reductions* (Washington: Brookings,1988).
- McCall, Malcolm & Ramsbotham, Oliver (eds.), *Just Deterrence: Morality and Deterrence in the Twenty-First Century* (London: School of Peace Studies, University of Bradford Press,1989).
- McCormick, Richard & Ramsey, Paul (eds.), *Doing Evil to Achieve Good: Moral Choice in Conflict Situations* (Chicago: Loyola University Press, 1978).
- McElroy, Robert W., *Morality and the American Foreign Policy: The Role of Ethics in International Relations* (Princeton: Princeton University Press, 1992).
- McNamara, Robert S., *Out of the Cold: New Thinking for American Foreign and Defence Policy in the Twenty First Century* (London: Bloomsbury, 1990).
- McSorley, Richard S. J., *Kill? For Peace?* (Washington: Center for Peace Studies,1977).

- Melzer,Y., *Concept of Just War* (New York: Sijthoff, 1975).
- Merton, T., *Faith and Violence: Christian Teaching and Christian Practice* (Notre Dame: University of Notre Dame Press, 1968).
- Mill, John Stuart, *Dissertations and Discussions* (Boston: William V Spencer, 1867).
- Miller, Steven E. (ed.), *Strategy and Nuclear Deterrence: An International Security Reader* (Princeton, N.J.: Princeton University Press, 1984).
- Morgan, Patrick, *Deterrence: A Conceptual Analysis* (London: Sage, 1977).
- Morganthau, Hans, *Politics Among Nations* (New York: Alfred Knopf, 1967).
- Mueller, John (ed.), *Approaches to Measurements in International Relations* (New York: Appleton-Century-Crofts, 1969).
- Murnion, Philip J. (ed.), *Catholics and Nuclear War: A Commentary on Challenge of Peace – The U.S. Catholic Bishops Pastoral Letter on War and Peace* (New York: Crossroad, 1983).
- Murray, John Courtney, *Morality and Modern War* (New York: Council on Religious and International Affairs, 1959).
- — do —, *We Hold These Truths: Catholic Reflections on American Propositions* (New York: Sheed & Warne, 1960).
- Nacht, Michael, *The Age of Vulnerability* (Washington D.C.: Brookings, 1985).
- Nagle, John U., *War and Human Progress* (New York: W.W. Norton & Co., 1963).

- Nagle, William (ed.), *Morality and Modern Warfare* (Baltimore: Helicon Press, 1960).
- Niebuhr, Reinhold, *Christianity and Power Politics* (New York: Charles Scribner's Sons, 1990).
- Nisbet, Robert, *Twilight of Authority* (New York: Oxford University Press, 1975).
- Novak, Michael, *Moral Clarity in the Nuclear Age* (Nashville: Thomas Nelson, 1983).
- Nye, Joseph H., Jr., *Peace in Parts* (Boston: Little Brown, 1971).
- — do —, *The Making of America's Soviet Policy* (New Haven, Conn.: Yale University Press, 1984).
- — do —, *Nuclear Ethics* (New York: Free Press, 1986).
- — do —, *Bound to Lead: The Changing Nature of American Power* (New York: Basic Books, 1990).
- O'Brien, William V., *Nuclear War, Deterrence and in order of year Morality* (New York: Newman Press, 1967).
- O'Brien, David J., and Shannon, Thomas A. (eds.), *Renewing the Earth : Catholic Documents on Peace, Justice and Liberation* (N.Y. Garden city : Doubleday, 1977).
- — do —, *The Conduct of Just and Limited Wars* (New York: Praeger Publishers, 1981).
- — do — and Langan, John S.J., *The Nuclear Dilemma and the Just War Tradition* (Lexington, M.A.: Lexington Books,1986).
- Oppenheim, Felix E., *The Place of Morality* (Lexington, Mass. : D.C. Health & Co., 1991).
- Osgood, Charles, *An Alternative to War or Surrender* (Urbana: University of Illinois Press, 1962).

- Osgood, R.E. & Tucker, R.W., *Force, Order and Justice* (Baltimore : The John Hopkins University Press, 1967).
- Osterud, Oyvind, (ed.), *Studies of War and Peace* (Norway : Norwegian University Press, 1986).
- Phillips, R.I., *War and Justice* (Oklahoma : University of Oklahoma Press, 1984).
- Pipes, Richard, *Survival Is Not Enough* (New York : Simon & Schuster, 1984).
- Poole, Walter S., *The History of Joint Chiefs of Staff and National Policy,* Vol. 1, 1945-47, 4 Vols., (Wilmington Del.: Michael Glagier, 1977-1980).
- Poole, Robert W., Jr. (ed.), *Defending a Free Society* (Lexington Mass : Lexington Books, 1984).
- Potter, Ralph, B., *War and Moral Discourse* (Richmond, VA : John Knox Press, 1970).
- Powers, Thomas, *Thinking About the Next War* (New York : Knopf, 1982).
- Preston, Richard, Sydney, Wise and Werner, Herman, *Men in Arms : A History of Warfare and Its Interrelationship with Western Society* (N.Y. : Praeger, 1956).
- Pringle, Peter, and Arkin, William, *SIOP : The Secret US Plan for Nuclear War* (New York : W.W. Norton, 1983).
- Prins, Gwyn, (ed.), *The Choice : Nuclear Weapons Versus Security* (London : Chatto & Windus, 1984).
- Pearton, M., *The Knowledgeable State : Diplomacy, War and Technology Since 1830* (London : Burnett Books, 1983).
- Quester, George H., *The Future of Nuclear Deterrence* (Lexington, MA. : Lexington University Press, 1986).

- Ramsey, Paul, *War and Christian Conscience* (Durham, NG. : Duke University Press, 1961).
- — do —, *The Limits of Nuclear War : Thinking About the Doable and the Un-Doable* (New York : Council on Religious and International Affairs, 1963).
- — do —, *The Just War : Force and Political Responsibility* (New York : Charles Seribner's Sons, 1968).
- Rawls, John, *A Theory of Justice* (Cambridge : Harvard University Press, 1971).
- Rizopoulos, Nicholas, *Sea Changes : American Foreign Policy in a World Transformed* (New York : Council on Foreign Relations Press, 1990).
- Rosenau, James (ed.), *In Search of Global Patterns* (New York : Free Press, 1976).
- Rostow, Eugene W., *Towards Managed Peace : The National Security Interests of the United States, 1759 to the Present* (New Haven, Conn : Yale University Press, 1993).
- Rotblat, Joseph, Steinbrunner, Jack & Balachandra, U. (eds.), *The Zero Option: A Nuclear Weapon Free World* (*Boulder,* Co.: Westview Press, 1993).
- Russell, Frederick H., *The Just War in the Middle Ages* (New York : Cambridge University Press, 1975).
- Russett, Bruce and Starr, Harvey, *World Politics : The Menu for Choice* (San Francisco: W.R. Freeman & Co., 1981).
- Russett, B., *The Prisoners of Insecurity* (San Francisco: W.R. Freeman & Co., 1983).
- Sagan, Scott D., *Moving Targets : Nuclear Strategy and National Security* (Princeton : Princeton University Press, 1989).

- Scheer, Robert, *With Enough Shovels : Reagon, Bush and Nuclear War* (London : Secker & Warburg, 1982).
- Schell, Jonathan, *The Fate of the Earth* (New York: Knopf., 1982).
- — do —, *The Abolition* (New York : Knopf, 1984).
- Schelling, Thomas, *Arms and Influence* (New Haven, Conn. : Yale University, 1961).
- — do —, *The Strategy of Conflict* (New York : Oxford University Press, 1963).
- Schwartz, David N., *NATO's Nuclear Dilemmas* (Washington, D.C. : Brookings Institution, 1983).
- Schwarzenberger, George, *International Law*, Vol. II, *The Law of Armed Conflict* (Abingdon Professional Books, 1976).
- Shannon, Thomas, A., (ed.), *War or Peace? The Search for New Answers* (New York, Maryknoll : Orbis, 1980).
- — do —, *What Are They Saying About Peace and War* (New York : Paulist Press, 1983).
- Sherwin, Martin J., *A World Destroyed : The Atomic Bomb and the Atlantic Alliance* (New York : Vintage Books, 1979).
- Shue, Henry (ed.), *Nuclear Deterrence and Moral Restraint : Critical Choices for American Strategy* (New York: Cambridge University Press, 1989).
- Sims, N.A., *Explorations in Ethics and International Relations* (London : Croom Helm, 1981).
- Smith, Charles Durya, (ed.), *The Hundred Percent Challenge : Building a National Institute of Peace : A Platform for Planning and Programs* (Washington D.C. : Seven Locks Press, 1985).

- Smoke, Richard, *National Security and Nuclear Dilemma* (Reading MA : Addison-Wesley Publishing Co., 1984).
- Snyder, Glenn H., *Deterrence and Defense : Towards a Theory of National Security* (Princeton, NJ. : Princeton University Press, 1961).
- — do —, *The Ideology of the Offensive* (Ithaca, N.Y. : Cornell University Press, 1984).
- — do — & Diesing, Paul, *Conflict Among Nations : Bargaining, Decision-Making and System Structure in International Crisis* (Princeton, N.J.: Princeton University Press, 1977).
- Spaeth Robert L., *No Easy Answers : Christians Debate Nuclear Arms* (Minnesota : Minnesota Winston Press, 1983).
- Spanier, John W., *American Foreign Policy Since World War II,* 8th edn.(New York : Holt Reinhart & Winston, 1984).
- Speed, Roger D., *Strategic Deterrence in the 1980s* (Palo Alto, CA. : Hoover Institution Press, 1979).
- Sterba, James P., *The Ethics of War and Nuclear Deterrence* (Belmont : California : Wordsworth, 1985).
- Stimson, Henry L & Bundy, McGeorge, *On Active Service in Peace & War* (London : Hutchinson, 1948).
- Stoesinger, John G., *Crusaders and Pragmatists : Movers of Modern American Foreign Policy* (New York : W.W. Norton & Co., 1979).
- — do —, *Why Nations Go to War,* 3rd edn. (New York : St. Martin's Press, 1982).
- Stone, Jeremy, *Strategic Persuasion* (New York : Colombia University Press, 1967).

- Stone, Julius, *Aggression and World Order* (London : Stevens & Sons, 1958).
- Strauss, Leo, *Natural Right and History* (Chicago : University of Chicago Press, 1953).
- Suarez, Francisco, *The Classics of International Law* (Selections from the three works of F. Suarez, S.J.) Vol.II, No.20 (Oxford : Clarendon Press, 1944).
- Tarr, David, *American Strategy in the Nuclear Age* (New York : Macmillan, 1966).
- Taylor, Maxwell, *D., Precarious Security* (New York: Norton, 1976).
- Tedder, Arthur William, Lord, *Air Power in War* (London: Hodder & Stoughton, 1947).
- Thompson, C.S. (ed.), *Morals and Missiles* (London : James Clarke & Co., 1959).
- Thompson, E.P., *Zero Option* (London : Merlin Press, 1982).
- Thompson, Kenneth W., *Christian Ethics and Dilemma of Foreign Policy* (Durham, NC. : Duke University Press, 1959).
- — do —, *Moral Dimensions of American Foreign Policy* (New Brunswick, N.J. Transaction Books, 1984).
- Tsipis, Kosta, *Arsenal* : *Understanding Weapons in the Nuclear Age* (New York : Simon & Schuster, 1983).
- Tucker, Robert W., *The Just War : A Study of Contemporary American Doctrine* (Baltimore The John Hopkins University Press, 1960).
- — do —, *The Nuclear Debate : Deterrence and the Lapse of Faith* (New York : Holmes and Meier, 1985).
- Ulam, Adam., *The Rivals : America and Russia Since World War II* (New York : Penguin Books, 1980).

- Vance, Cyrus, *Hard Choice : Critical Years in American Foreign Policy* (New York : Simon & Schuster, 1983).
- Walzer, Michael, *Just and Unjust Wars : A Moral Argument with Historical Illustrations* (New York : Basic Books, 1977).
- Walker, R.B.J., *One World, Many Worlds : Struggles for a Just World Peace* (Boulder : Lynn Reinner, 1988).
- Wasserstrom, Richard A. (ed.), *War and Morality* (Balmont CA. : Wordsworth Publication Co., 1970).
- Weeks, Albert L., & Bodie, William C. (eds.), *War and Peace : Soviet Russia Speaks* (Washington : National Strategy Information Centre, 1983).
- Weston, Burns, H. (ed.), *Towards Nuclear Disarmament and Global Security : A Search for Alternatives* (Boulder, Colo : Westview Press, 1984).
- — do —, *Alternative Security : Living Without Nuclear Deterrence* (Boulder : Westview Press, 1990).
- White, Ralph, *Nobody Wanted War* (Garden City, New York : Doubleday, 1968).
- Williams, Bernard, *Ethics and the Limits of Philosophy* (Cambridge : Harvard University Press, 1985).
- Windaas, Stanley, *Christianity Versus Violence: A Social and Historical Study of War and Christianity* (London : Sheed and Ward, 1964).
- Winters, Francis X., S.J., *Politics and Ethics* (New York: Paulist Press, 1975).
- Wolin, Sheldon *S., Politics and Vision* (Boston: Little Brown, 1960).
- Wong, Fraser and Agatha, S.Y., *Symmetry and Selectivity in US Defense Policy: Grand Design or a Major Mistake* (Lanham, Md.: University Press of America, 1983).

- Woolsey, James R. (ed.), *Nuclear Arms : Ethics, Strategy, Politics* (San Fransisco: ICS Press, 1984).
- Wright, Quincy, *A Study of War* (Chicago: University of Chicago Press, 1942).
- York, Herbert E., *Race to Oblivion: A Participant's View of the Arms Race* (New York: Simon & Schuster, 1970).
- — do —, *The Advisors: Oppenheimer, Teller and the Superbomb* (San Fransisco, CA.: WH Freeman, 1976).
- Zahn, Gordon C., *An Alternative to War* (New York: Council on Religious & International Affairs, 1963).
- — do —, *War, Conscience and Dissent* (New York: Hawthorn, 1967).
- Ziegler, David W., *War, Peace and International Politics,* 2nd edn. *(Boston: Little Brown & Co., 1981).*
- Zuckerman, Solly, Lord, *Nuclear Illusion and Reality* (London : Collins, 1982).

Articles and Papers

- Achen, Christopher H. and Duncan, Snydel, "Rational Deterrence Theory and Comparative Case Studies", *World Politics* 41 (January 1989), pp.143-169.
- Arbatov, G.A., "The American Strategic Debate: A Soviet View", *Survival* 16 (May/June 1964).
- Ball, Desmond, "Can Nuclear War be Controlled?", *Adelphi Paper 169* (London: IISS, 1980), Sec.V.
- — do —, "Targeting for Strategic Deterrence", *AdelphiPaper 180* (London: IISS, 1983).
- — do —, " U.S. Strategic Forces: How Should They be Used?", *International Security*, Vol. 7, No.3 (Winter 1982-83), pp.31-60.

- — do — and Toth, Robert C., "Revising the SIOP", *International Security* Vol.14, No.4 (Spring 1980), pp.65-92.
- Berns, Walter, "The New Pacifism and World Government", *National Review*, 27 May 1983, pp.613-620.
- Blight, James G., "The New Psychology of War and Peace", *International Security*, Vol. 11, No.3 (Winter 1986-1987), pp. 175-186.
- Brennan, Donald George, "Strategy and Conscience", *Bulletin of Atomic Scientists*, Vol.21, No. 10 (December 1985), pp.27-28.
- — do —, "The Case for Missile Defence", *Foreign Affairs*, Vol.47, No.3 (April 1969), pp.433-448.
- Brodie, Bernard, "The Anatomy of Deterrence", *World Politics*, Vol.II (January 1959), pp.173-192.
- — do —, "On Clausewitz: A Passion for War", *World Politics* 25 (January 1973), pp.288-308.
- — do —, "The Development of Nuclear Strategy", *International Security*, Vol.2, No.4 (Spring 1978), pp.65-83.
- Brown, Harold, "The Objective of U.S. Strategic Forces", *Survival* (November-December 1980), pp.267-269.
- Builder, Carl, "The Prospects and Implications of Non-Nuclear Means for Strategic Conflict", *Adelphi Paper 200* (London: IISS, 1985).
- Bundy, McGeorge, "To Cap the Volcano", *Foreign Affairs*, Vol.48, No.1 (October 1969), pp.1-20.
- — do —, Kennan, George F., McNamara, R.S. & Smith, G., "Nuclear Weapons and the Atlantic Alliance",

Foreign Affairs, Vol.60, No.4 (Spring 1982), pp.753-768.

- Burns, Arthur Lee, "Ethics and Deterrence", *Adelphi Paper 69* (London: IISS, 1970).
- Bush, George, "George Bush and Arms Control: The Question in 1992", *Arms Control Today,* Vol.22, No.3 (April 1992), pp.3-5.
- Brzezinski, Z., "The Cold War and its Aftermath" *Foreign Affairs,* Vol.71, No.4 (Fall 1992), pp.31-49.
- Cahill, Lisa Sowle,"Taleology, Utilitarianism and Christian Ethics", *Theological Studies,* 42 (1981), pp.601-629.
- Carter, Barry, "Nuclear Strategy and Nuclear Weapons", *Scientific American,* 230 (May 1974), pp.20-31.
- Chernoff, F., "Ending the Cold War: Soviet Retreat and The Military Build-Up, *International Affairs,* Vol.67, No.1 (1991), pp.111-126.
- Clarke, Duncan F., "Arms Control and Foreign Policy Under Reagan", *The Bulletin of Atomic Scientists* (November 1981), pp.12-19.
- Clarke, William, "High Frontier", *Newsweek* , April 4, 1993.
- Claude, I., "Just War Doctrine and Institutions", *Political Science Quarterly,* Vol.95, No.1 (Spring 1980), pp.83-96.
- Cohen, E., "The Future of Force", *The National Interest,* 21 (Fall 1990), pp.3-15.
- Dean, Jonathan, "Beyond First-Use", *Foreign Policy,* No.48 (Fall 1982), pp.37-53.
- D'Estang, Valery Giscard, Nakasone, Y. and Kissinger, H., "East-West Relations", *Foreign Affairs,* Vol.68, No.3 (Summer 1989), pp.1-21.

- Draper, Theodore, "How Not to Think About Nuclear War", *New York Review of Books,* XXIX, No.12 , July 15, 1982, pp.35-41.
- — do —, "Dear Mr. Weinberger: An Open Reply to an Open Letter", *New York Review of Books,* XXIX, No.17, November 4, 1982, p.26 ff.
- Drell, Sydney, Hippel, Frank Von and Holloway, D., "Preserving the ABM Treaty: A Critique of the Reagan Strategic Defense Initiative", *International Security,* Vol 9, No.2 (Autumn 1984), pp.51-91.
- Dougherty, William and Levi, "The Consequences of Limited Nuclear Attacks on the U.S.", *International Security,* Vol.10, No.4 (Spring 1986), pp.3-45.
- Downs, George, Rocke, David and Siverson, Randolph, "Arms Race and Cooperation", *World Politcs* 38 (October 1985), pp.134-43.
- Downs, George W., "The Rational Deterrence Debate", *World Politics* (January 1989), pp.225-237.
- Feiveson, Herald A., Ullman, Richard H. and Hippel, Frank Von, "Reducing U.S. and Soviet Nuclear Arsenals", *Bulletin of Atomic Scientists,* XLI (1985), pp.144-150.
- Fetter, Steve, "Ballistic Missiles and Weapons of Mass Destruction: What Should be Done?", *International Security,* Vol.1, No.1 (Summer 1991), pp.5-42.
- Fink, Clinton, "More Calculations About Deterrence", *Journal of Conflict Resolution 9* (March 1965), pp.54-65.
- Ford, John C., "The Morality of Obliteration Bombing", *Theological Studies* 5 (September 1944), pp.261-309.

- Freedman, Lawrence, "Indignation, Influence and Strategic Studies", *International Affairs,* Vol.60, No.2 (Spring 1984), pp.207-19.
- — do —, "Strategic Defence in the Nuclear Age", *Adelphi Paper 224* (London: IISS, 1987).
- — do —, "Does Deterrence Have a Future?", *Arms Control Today* (October 2000), pp.3-8.
- Gaddis, John Lewis, "The Long Peace", *International Security,* Vol.10, No.4 (Spring 1986), pp.99-142.
- Garfinkle, Adam M., "The Unmaking of the Nuclear Freeze", *Washington Quarterly* (Spring 1985), pp.109-120.
- — do —, "The Attack on Deterrence: Reflections on Morality and Strategic Praxis", *Journal of Strategic Studies* (June 1989), pp.166-195.
- George, A. L. and Smoke, R., " Deterrence and Foreign Policy", *World Politics,* 41 (January 1989), pp.170-182.
- Gessert, Robert A., "P.D.-59: The Better Way", *Worldview,* Vol. 23, No.1 (November 1980), pp.7-12.
- Glaser, Charles L., "Why Even Good Defenses May be Bad?", *International Security,* Vol.9, No.2 (Fall 1984), pp.92-123.
- — do —, "Nuclear Policy Without an Adversary: U.S. Planning for Post-Soviet Era", *International Security,* Vol.16, No. 4 (Spring 1992), pp.34-78.
- Goodwin, Robert E., "Nuclear Disarmament as a Moral Certainty", *Ethics* (March 1985).
- Gouré, Daniel, "Nuclear Deterrence: Then and Now", Policy Review Online, www.policyreview.org/dec02/goure.html.

- Gray, Colin S., "The Arms Race Phenomenon", *World Politics* 24 (October 1971), pp.39-79.
- — do —, "The Arms Race is About Politics", *Foreign Policy* (Winter 1972-73).
- — do —, "The Urge to Compete: Rationale for Arms Racing", *World Politics,* Vol.26, No.2 (January 1974).
- — do —, "Nuclear Strategy : A Case for a Theory of Victory", *International Security,* Vol.1, No.4 (Summer 1979).
- — do —, "Targeting Problems for Central War", *Naval War College Review,* Vol.33, No.1 (January-February 1980), pp.3-21.
- — do —, "War Fighting for Deterrence", *Journal of Strategic Studies,* Vol.7, No.1 (March 1984), pp.5-28.
- Gray Colin S., & Payne, Keith "Under the Nuclear Gun: Victory is possible," *Foreign Policy,* No. 39 (Summer 1980), pp.14-27.
- — do —, "Nuclear Policy and the Defensive Transition", *Foreign Affairs,* Vol.62, No.4 (Spring 1984), pp.820-842.
- Greenwood, Ted and Nacht, Michael L., "The New Nuclear Debate: Sense or Nonsense?", *Foreign Affairs* 52 (July 1974), pp.761-780.
- Grisez, Germain, "Moral Implications of a Nuclear Deterrent", *Centre Journal* 2 (1982-1983), pp.9-24.
- Halperin, Morton, "The Good, The Bad, The Wasteful", *Foreign Policy 6* (Spring 1972), pp.69-83.
- Hardin, Russell, "Unilateral Versus Mutual Disarmament", *Philosophy and Public Affairs 12* (1983), pp.236-54.

- Hehir, Bryan J., "New Issues in an Old Argument", *Worldview,* Vol. 23, No.11 (November 1980), pp.7-12.
- — do —, "Just War Theory in a Post Cold War World", *The Journal of Religious Ethics,* Vol.20, No.2 (Fall 1992), pp.237-57.
- Herz, John, "Idealist Internationalism and the Security Dilemma", *World Politcs2* (January 1950), pp.157-80.
- Hendrickson, David, "The Renovation of American Foreign Policy", *Foreign Afairs,* Vol.71, No.2 (Spring 1992), pp.48-63.
- Hines, John G., Peterson, Philip A. and Tulock, Notra III, "Soviet Military Theory from 1945-2000: Implications for NATO", *Washington Quarterly,* Vol.9, No. 4 (Fall 1986), pp.117-37.
- Howard, Michael, "The Concept of Peace: On Its Illusion and Achievements", *Encounter,* Vol. 16, No.4 (December 1982), pp.18-24.
- — do —, "Reassurance and Deterrence: Western Defense in the 1980s", *Foreign Affairs,* Vol.61, No.2 (Winter 1982-83), pp.309-24.
- Huth, Paul, "Extended Deterrence and the Outbreak of War", *American Political Science Review* 82 (June 1988), pp.423-44.
- — do — and Russett, B., "Deterrence : Failure and Escalation", *International Studies Quarterly,* Vol. 32, No. 1 (March 1988), pp. 29-46.
- — do — "What Makes Deterrence Work: Cases From 1900-1980", *World Politics* Vol. 36, No. 4 (July 1984), pp.496-526.
- Ikle, Fred, "Can Nuclear Deterrence Last Out the Century?", *Foreign Affairs,* Vol.1, No.1 (1973), pp.267-285.

- — do —, "Nuclear Strategy: Can There Be A Happy Ending?", *Foreign Affairs*, Vol.63, No.4(Spring 1985), pp.810-826.
- Jervis, Robert, "Cooperation Under the Security Dilemma", *World Politics*, Vol. 30, No. 2 (January 1978), pp.167-214.
- — do —, "Deterrence and Perception", *International Security*, Vol.7, No. 3 (Winter 1982-83), pp.3-30.
- — do —, "From Balance to Concert: A Study of International Security Cooperation", *World Politics*, Vol. 38, No. 1 (October 1985): 58-79.
- — do —, "Rational Deterrence : Theory and Evidence", *World Politics*, Vol. 41, No. 2 (January 1989), pp.183-207.
- Johnson, J.T., "On Keeping Faith: The Uses of History for Religious Ethics", *Journal of Religious Ethics*,Vol.7, No.1 (Spring 1979), pp.98-116.
- Kaiser, Karl, Leber, George Mertes Alois, Schultze, F. J., "Nuclear Weapons and the Preservation of Peace: Response to an American Proposal for Renouncing the First-Use of Nuclear Weapons", *Foreign Affairs*,Vol.60, No.5 (Summer 1982), pp.1157-70.
- Kaplan, Morton, "The Calculus of Nuclear Deterrence", *World Politics*, Vol .2, No.1 (October 1958), pp.20-43.
- Keeny, Spurgeon M and Panofsky, Wolfgang, "MAD Versus NUTS: Can Doctrine of Weaponry Remedy the Mutual Hostage Relationship of the Super Powers?", *Foreign Affairs*, Vol. 60, No.2 (Winter 1981-82), pp.287-304.
- Kaufmann, W.W., "The Crisis in Military Affairs", *World Politics*, Vol.10, No.4 (July 1958), pp.579-603.

- Krauthammer, Charles, "The Obsolescence of Deterrence", *The Weekly Standard,* http://www.theweeklystandard.com/default.asp
- Kull, Steven, "Nuclear Nonsense", *Foreign Policy,* Vol.58 (Spring 1985), pp.28-52.
- Lackay, Douglas, "Missiles and Morals: A Utilitarian Look at Nuclear Deterrence", *Philosophy and Public Affairs,*11 (1982), pp.189-231.
- Langan, John S.J., "The American Hierarchy and Nuclear Weapons", *Theological Studies* 43 (1982).
- Lebow, Richard Ned, "Windows of Opportunity: Do States Jump Through Them?", *International Security,* Vol.9, No.1 (Summer 1984), pp.147-186.
- — do —, and Gross Stein, Janice, "Deterrence : The Elusive Dependent Variable", *World Politics,* Vol. 42, No.3 (April 1990), pp.336-369.
- — do —, "Rational Deterrence Theory: I Think Therefore I Deter", *World Politics,* Vol.41, No.2 (January 1989), pp.208-224.
- Luard, Evan, "Conciliation and Deterrence: A Comparison of Political Strategies in the Interwar and Postwar Periods", *World Politics,* Vol.19, No.2 (January 1967), pp.183-187.
- Luttwak, Edward N., "How to Think About Nuclear War", *Commentary* 74 (August 1982), pp.21-28.
- Maxwell, Stephen, "Rationality in Deterrence", *Adelphi Papers* 50 (London:IISS, August 1968), pp.4-7.
- May, Michael M.,"Some Advantages of a Counterforce Deterrence", *Orbis* 14 (Summer 1970), pp.271-283.
- McNamara, Robert, "The Military Role of Nuclear Weapons: Perceptions and Misperceptions", *Foreign Affairs,* Vol.62, No.1 (Fall 1983), pp.59-80.

- Mearsheimer, John J., "Back to the Future: Instability in Europe After the Cold War", *International Security,* Vol.16, No.1 (Summer 1990), pp.5-56.
- Nitze, Paul, "On the Road to a More Stable Peace", Speech before the Philadelphia World Affairs Council, Philadelphia, Penn, reprint in *Energy and Technology Review* (February 1987), pp. 9-11 (Washington D.C.: State Department, February 20, 1985).
- Novak, Michael, "Arms and the Church", *Commentary,* March 9, 1982.
- — do —, "Nuclear Morality", *America,* July 3, 1982.
- Nye, Joseph S. (Jr.), "What New World Order?", *Foreign Affairs,* Vol.71, No.2 (Spring 1992), pp.83-96.
- O'Brien, William W., "The Bishop's Unfinished Business", *Comparative Strategy,* Vol.5, No.2 (1985), pp.105-133.
- Okin, Susan Moller, "Taking the Bishops Seriously", *World Politics,* Vol.36, No.4(July 1984), pp.527-554.
- Paul II, Pope John Paul, "Address to Drogedha (Ireland)", *Origins 9* (1979), pp.272-275.
- — do —, "World Peace Day Message", *Origins 11* (1982), pp.473-78.
- Payne, Keith B., "Post-Cold War Requirements for U.S. Nuclear Deterrence Policy", *Comparative Strategy 17* (July-September 1998), pp.227-277.
- Rappaport, Annatole, "The Source of Anguish", *Bulletin of Atomic Scientists,* Vol.21, No.10 (December 1965), pp.31-32.
- Reagan's Speech, *Deadalus,* Vol.114, No.3 (Summer 1983). Also in *New York Times,* March 24, 1983.

- Risse-Kappen, T., "Did Peace Through Strength End the Cold War?: Lessons from INF", *International Security,* Vol.16, No.1 (Summer 1991), pp.162-188.
- Rogers, Bernard, "Arms Control and Deterrence", *Global Affairs,* Vol. 3, No.1 (Winter 1988), pp.1-15.
- Rosecrance, Richard, "A New Concert of Power", *Foreign Affairs,* Vol.71, No.2 (Spring 1992), pp.64-82.
- Rosenberg, David, "American Atomic Strategy and the Hydrogen Bomb", *Journal of American History 66* (June 1979).
- — do —, "U.S. Nuclear Stockpile: 1945-1950", *The Bulletin of Atomic Scientists,* Vol.38, No.5 (May 1982), pp.25-30.
- — do —, "The Origins of Overkill: Nuclear Weapons and American Strategy–1945-1960", *International Security,* Vol. 7, No. 4 (Spring 1983), pp.3-71.
- — do —, "A Smoking Radiating Ruin at the End of Two Hours: Documents of American Plans for Nuclear War with the Soviet Union, 1954-55", *International Security,* Vol.6, No.3 (Winter 1981/82), pp.3-38.
- Russett, Bruce, "The Calculus of Deterrence", *Journal of Conflict Resolution,* Vol.7, No.3 (June 1963), pp.97-109.
- Sagan, Scott,"Nuclear Alerts and Crisis Management", *International Security,* Vol. 9, No.4 (Spring 1985), pp.99-139.
- — do —, "1914 Revisited", *International Security,* Vol. 11, No.2 (Fall 1980), pp.151-75.
- Schelling, Thomas G., "What Went Wrong With Arms Control?" *Foreign Affairs* 64 (Winter 1985-86), pp.219-233.

- — do —, "The Impact of Nuclear Weapons in History", *Washington Quarterly*, Vol.16, No.2 (Autumn 1992), pp.5-12.
- Schlesinger, Arthur, "The Origins of the Cold War", *Foreign Affairs* (October 1967), pp.22-52.
- Scoville, Herbert Jr., "Flexible Madness?", *Foreign Policy* No.14 (Spring 1974), pp.164-177.
- Snyder, Glenn, "Deterrence and Power", *Journal of Conflict Resolution*, Vol. 4, No. 2 (June 1960), pp.163-178.
- Steinbrunner, John D., "Beyond Rational Deterrence: The Struggle for New Concept", *World Politics*, Vol. 28, No.4 (January 1976), pp.223-245.
- — do —, "Nuclear Decapitation", *Foreign Policy*, No. 45 (Winter 1981-82), pp.16-28.
- Stockton, Paul N., "The New Game on the Hill: The Politics of Arms Control, and Strategic Force Modernization", *International Security*, Vol.16, No.2 (Fall 1991), pp.146-170.
- Strachan, H., "Deterrence Theory: The Problems of Continuity", *Journal of Strategic Studies*, Vol.7 (December 1984), pp.394-405.
- Taylor, Maxwell, "The Legitimate Claims of National Security", *Foreign Affairs*, Vol.52, No.3 (April 1974), pp.577-594.
- Taylor, Theodore B., "Third Generation Nuclear Weapons", *Scientific American*, Vol. 256, No.4 (April 1987), pp.30-39.
- Thompson, Loren, "How to Stop Worrying and Love the Bomb", *Wall Street Journal*, March 17, 2002.

- Tsipis, Kosta, "The Accuracy of Strategic Missiles", *Scientific American,* Vol.233 (July 1975), pp.14-23.
- Van Evera, Stephen, "The Cult of the Offensive and the Origins of the First War", *International Security,* Vol.9, No.1 (Summer 1984).
- Waltz, Kenneth, "The Spread of Nuclear Weapons: More May be Better?", *Adelphi Paper* 171 (London: IISS, 1981).
- Weinberger, Casper, "Open Letter to Thirty U.S. and Forty Foreign Publications", *New York Review of Books,* Vol.XXIX, No.17, November 4, 1982, p.27.
- Weiszacker, Carl and Friedrich Von , "Can a Third World War be Prevented?", *International Security,* Vol.5, No.1 (Summer 1980), pp.198-205.
- Wells, Donald A., "How Much Can the Just War Justify?", *The Journal of Philosophy,* Vol.66, No.23 (December 1969), pp.819-29.
- Wohlstetter, Albert, "The Delicate Balance of Terror", *Foreign Affairs,* Vol.17, No.2 (January 1959), pp.211-34.
- — do ——, "Bishops, Statesmen and Other Strategists on the Bombing of Innocents", *Commentary* (June 1983), pp.15-35.
- — do —, "Between the Unfree World and None: Increasing Our Choice", *Washington Quarterly,* Vol.9, No.4 (Fall 1986), pp.117-130 and in *Foreign Affairs,* Vol.63, No.5 (Spring 1985).
- X (G. F. Kennan), "The Sources of Soviet Conduct", *Foreign Affairs,* Vol.25, No.4 (July 1947), pp.566-582.
- Zuberi, M., "Scientists, Social Scientists and the State of Nuclear Terror", *Man and Development* (September 1986), pp.28-34.

- — do —, "Nuclear Arms Control", *World Focus* (May 1993).

Newspapers

- Asmus, R.D., "An Outward Looking New NATO or No NATO At All", *International Herald Tribune,* April 13, 1993, p.6.
- Leghorn, Col Richard S., "No Need to Bomb Cities to Win Wars: A New Counterforce Strategy for Air Warfare", *U.S. News and World Report,* January 28, 1955.
- Mahon, Michael S.J., "Nuclear Morality: A Primer for the Perplexed", *National Jesuit News* (November 1982).
- Toth, Robert C., "U.S. Scratches Nuclear Targets in Soviet Bloc", *Los Angeles Times,* April 19, 1991.

Index